MW01156841

SERVING IN
YOUR CHURCH
MUSIC MINISTRY

OTHER TITLES IN THE ZONDERVAN PRACTICAL MINISTRY GUIDE SERIES

Serving in the Praying Church, Charles E. Lawless Jr.
Serving as a Church Greeter, Leslie Parrott
Serving as a Church Usher, Leslie Parrott
Serving in the Church Nursery, Julia A. Spohrer
Serving in Church Visitation, Jerry M. Stubblefield
Serving by Safeguarding Your Church, Robert H. Welch

Paul E. Engle is an executive editor and associate publisher for editorial development at Zondervan. He has served as a pastor and as an instructor in several seminaries. Among the eight books he has written are *Baker's Wedding Handbook*, *Baker's Funeral Handbook*, and *God's Answers for Life's Needs*.

Randall D. Engle is senior pastor and director of music at the North Hills Christian Reformed Church of Troy, Michigan. He holds degrees from Calvin College, Calvin Theological Seminary, and Luther Seminary and is working on a Ph.D. at the University of Wales. He is the author of *So You've Been Asked to Lead Congregational Singing*.

SERVING IN YOUR CHURCH MUSIC MINISTRY

PAUL E. ENGLE, SERIES EDITOR

RANDALL D. ENGLE

ZONDERVAN™

GRAND RAPIDS, MICHIGAN 49530 USA

ZONDERVAN™

Serving in Your Church Music Ministry
Copyright © 2002 by Randall D. Engle

Requests for information should be addressed to:

Zondervan, *Grand Rapids, Michigan 49530*

Library of Congress Cataloging-in-Publication Data

Engle, Randall D., 1965–
     Serving in your church music ministry / Randall D. Engle.
          p.   cm. — (Zondervan practical ministry guides)
     Includes bibliographical references.
        ISBN 0-310-24101-4
        1. Church music — Handbooks, manuals, etc.   I. Title.   II. Series.
     ML3001 .E56   2002
     264' .2 — dc21

                                                                2002007824

Interior design by Sherri Hoffman

Printed in the United States of America

---

02 03 04 05 06 07 08 /❖ DC/ 10 9 8 7 6 5 4 3 2 1

For my parents, Verland and Jean,
whose faithful observance of the Lord's Day
taught me to love to worship

CONTENTS

Acknowledgments   9

Preface   11

1. **Words on Worship**   13
   Work Worthy of Eternity
   Entertaining God
   Who's at the Center?
   Worship Leaders Point Us to the Throne
   Yes! We'll ALL Gather at the River
   "I Believe in the Communion of Saints"
   Questions for Reflection and Discussion

2. **Planning for Worship**   21
   I'm Dreaming of a Sunday When . . .
   Church Leaders Unite!
   Questions for Reflection and Discussion

3. **Serving at the Keyboard**   33
   Worthy Is Christ!
   Survey Says . . .
   Back to the Basics: Musical Trust or Bust
   More Musical Trust
   God Is in the Details
   Organists
   Pianists
   Keyboardists
   Praying Twice
   Questions for Reflection and Discussion

4. **Serving with Your Voice**   47
    The Center of Praise: Our Song
    The Choir
    The Praise Team
    The Soloist
    The Children's Choir
    Questions for Reflection and Discussion

5. **Serving with an Instrument**   67
    Let Everything That Has Breath Praise the Lord!
    Brass Instruments
    Stringed Instruments
    Handbells
    Woodwind Instruments
    Guitars
    Harpsichords
    Percussion Instruments
    More Ideas!
    Questions for Reflection and Discussion

6. **Serving in the Pew**   77
    How to Worship Well with Heart and Mind
    How to Sing Well
    Questions for Reflection and Discussion

Appendix 1: A Church Musician's Prayer   87

Appendix 2: Worship Planning Checklist   89

Appendix 3: Instrumentalists' Survey   93

ACKNOWLEDGMENTS

This little book project has been a joy—supported and cheered by many.

I thank my editor Paul Engle (I still think we *must* be related), who called upon me and challenged me to do such a project.

I want to thank my wife, Kathy, and children, Jonathan and Elizabeth, who are with me on this wonderful journey of life. I love you all, both on even and odd days.

Colleagues like John Witvliet, John Ferguson, Mel Hugen, Anton Armstrong, Brent Assink, and Pat Hammink have challenged my theology of worship and honed my ideas. You are all God's gift to me. Thanks for long car rides of conversation, inspiring hymn playing, G&Ts, E-mails, Squash games, and long lunches (respectively)—and for being friends to a stiff-necked person like me. My coworker Anita Beem graces me with her presence each day and also graced the rough pages of this manuscript. And Adela Ringling, choir president par excellence, could write a manual on how to best befriend and support a choir director.

I must especially acknowledge with gratitude the Rev. Dr. Duane Kelderman, vice president of administration at Calvin Theological Seminary, who began mentoring me in my early years of seminary and continues to do so today. You have given to me in every way as I continue to develop as musician, worship planner, preacher, and pastor. You have made a difference, and I thank you. But then again, what did I expect of someone from Oskaloosa, Iowa?

Most of all, it is my hope that God would use this book, not to point to me, but to point to the One who sits on the throne.

—Rev. Randall D. Engle

PREFACE

A wise teacher of preachers once quipped that poor speakers ask, "What shall I say?" but good speakers ask, "Who is my audience?" Indeed, key to all communicative projects, including this book, is finding a voice and reaching the targeted audience.

That said, I need buckshot to hit my target. I'm writing to musicians and encouragers of musicians, to church employees and church volunteers, to ministry professionals and persons who just got the assignment to "run the worship program" at their church, to independent churches and churches that belong to denominations of all stripes, and to churches whose worship style runs the gamut from storefront gospel to high Latin Mass! All of this without being too technical on the one hand, or too simplistic and general on the other. I hope my aim is good and, if you can excuse the oxymoron, both broad and specific so that all persons and churches will be equally fortified and inspired to better ministry.

More than that, I also want to offer something new. I am aware of all the excellent academic texts and journals that exist in liturgics, church music, choir directing, improvisation, service planning, and so forth. However, in most publications, theory and practice often exist across a great divide. Either one hears from academics, who, quite honestly, have little experience working for a volunteer, not-for-profit organization (the church), or one hears from musicians and worship planners, whose ideas often have no theological rudder and whose writing remains only on the level of "a neat thing you might want to try."

What I have tried to do is to ground the duties (practice) of a church musician and worship planner in a biblical mandate for worship (theory). I want to knot theory and practice tightly together. In doing so I hope to stimulate musicians, artisans, preachers, worship planners and instrumentalists, Sunday school teachers—everyone who is connected in some way, shape, or form to the worship life of the church. I want us to look at worship and our role in it in different and new ways. I want to remind us all that our work has biblical precedent and that it is the conduit through which the Holy Spirit works to touch the lives and hearts of worshipers.

Our modern-day ethos puts me—you—in the center of everything: "We are the world!" "Be all you can be!" "You are the reason." When disorientation occurs about whom and what worship is for, battles erupt over music and worship style. And no one wins—not when discussions of worship begin and end by merely arguing personal preference. True worship renewal begins once congregants, pastors, and musicians agree that *worship is for God,* and when leaders and musicians begin making wise choices that flow from this basic premise. But the idea that worship is something first of all for God, not for me, sounds preposterous in a world of self-absorbed church shoppers.

Nevertheless, it is our calling to point worshipers to God. I pray that this little book will be useful to all stewards of music as we strive to do this.

ONE

Words on Worship

Come, we that love the Lord,
And let our joys be known;
Join in a song with sweet accord
And thus surround the throne,
And thus surround the throne.

Isaac Watts

WORK WORTHY OF ETERNITY

One Wednesday evening after choir rehearsal Jon and Joy grabbed their two daughters from the church nursery and slumped into the seats of their minivan, exhausted and spent. Tomorrow was a school day, and the hour was late. Jon had gone to church directly from the office, skipping dinner. They had spent all evening at church. After a quick stop at Caribou Coffee on the way home, Jon muttered to Joy, "Do you ever get tired of this? Frankly, this is one of those nights where I wonder whether it's worth it all. Maybe we should cut back and drop out of choir."

Joy was quick to respond. "I know how you feel, and tonight's not a good night to ask! But I came across an article this morning that helped change my whole attitude about music in church. The article pointed out that, in heaven, no earthly occupations will be needed, save one: church musicians. Think about it. In heaven doctors will have no clinics, for there will be only perfectly functioning and reenergized bodies. Lawyers and judges will have no reason to appear in court to settle disputes among people who are living together in peace. Even preachers will no longer need pulpits to win souls, for Christ will be living in the neighborhood, and we shall see Christ, and Christ shall be all in all!"

The article was right. For church musicians, earthly service comes with an implied eternal contract.

Given such a momentous task, church musicians ought to learn to worship well and lead worship well, for our worship here is a warm-up for the everlasting worship of God that is to come.

But what exactly is worship?

ENTERTAINING GOD

Worship is entertaining God. Worship celebrates God's greatness and his love for us. Worship receives God's word as it comes to us through the Bible, the sacraments (or ordinances), and Jesus Christ. It's clear that God desires and enjoys our worship and that God created all things to praise. The Bible says that all creatures give glory to God and that everything has its unique voice and mode of praise. Thunder, cattle, crickets, fruitful trees, and birds give glory to God (see Psalm 148)! One day even the trees of the fields will clack their branches together as though they were hands applauding the premiere of God's new creation. God delights in creation and in all of creation's worship. Worship entertains God.

Of all God's creatures, humans were created with a special role. Biblical authors hardly know how to express just how valuable we are to God other than to say that we were crowned with glory and honor and made just below the angels (Psalm

8:5). As the blue-ribbon prize of creation, God made us breathing, living instruments of praise. When we fill our lungs with air and breathe out through our vocal chords to shape words and phonate pitch, when we "play skillfully" (or not so skillfully) upon the harp (think "piano"), when we glide our bow across the fret of five-strings, the Spirit of God uses that to the delight of God.

Worship is explosive and life changing when we see it, not as a means to entertain us, but as a way to bring attention to God. God delights in creation's worship. I think God even whistles along with us in our praise of him!

WHO'S AT THE CENTER?

When we gather for worship, then, our attention should naturally be directed to God. Several times, when describing worship, the Bible's writers observe God at the center of worship. This makes sense, for worship exists to praise God, the One seated on the throne (Revelation 4:2). Worship does not first of all exist for us, but for God.

For example, when John has his vivid dream, which is recorded in the book of Revelation, he sees God seated on a throne (Revelation 4–5). This image is the center of the picture. Arching the throne is a jewel-studded rainbow comprised of rare and costly gems—imagine a ribbon of diamonds, emeralds, and rubies a block wide, miles long, and arching way up into the sky! Four living creatures are in a circle around the jewel-arched throne, each of these creatures representing the best of its species: the human (God's most amazing creature), the ox (the most humble of domesticated beasts), the eagle (the most skillful), and the lion (the boldest of creatures). In the next ring around the throne are twenty-four elders who bow down in worship. Around them assemble seas and seas of angels.

And then not only the four living creatures, not only the elders, not only the seas and seas of angels, but the *entire cosmos* gathers in the circle to bring a sevenfold ascription of praise to the One seated on the throne: "Worthy is the Lamb, who was slain, to receive power and wealth and wisdom and strength and honor and glory and praise!" (Revelation 5:12).

Everything defines its place in relationship to God's throne. Every note of praise and every organism find its place in relationship to God. Everything finds itself in God. Worship exists to bring praise to God, who is at the center.

WORSHIP LEADERS POINT US TO THE THRONE

Worship planners, leaders, and musicians use their skill and craft to point worshipers toward God. The role of keyboardists in worship is not to bedazzle the congregation with technical wizardry or to show how loudly the organ can be played, but rather to use music to bring people around the throne. Instrumentalists serve, not to focus attention on their instruments or on their graceful bowing techniques, but to invite the congregation to join an orchestra of sound that praises the Creator, Redeemer, and Sustainer. The purpose of soloists is not to flaunt an amazingly agile voice or to wallow in self-aggrandizing virtuosity, but to use words and music to invite worshipers to join their hearts and minds in praise of God. The purpose of worship planning is not to orchestrate liturgical acts into a laundry list of "must do" activities, but to facilitate all things so that attention points to God—and to what God is doing in worship, in our lives, and in our world. Liturgists and pastors are not emcees but facilitators used by the Spirit so that our attention naturally falls on God.

Worship celebrates God, who is at the center of life. Worship reminds us that God is on the throne, not us. Our worship and music point us to this reality.

YES! WE'LL <u>ALL</u> GATHER AT THE RIVER

Some churches have lost sight of the center of worship. Sadly, when God's throne is replaced at the center of worship, and when discussions about worship and music turn into discussions of preference, the point of worship is lost. For example, some churches are being torn apart by the worship wars. Part of the congregation wants to replace hymnals with screens on which words are projected, while another part suggests purchasing quickly the latest edition of their denomination's hymnal so that they'll have an excuse never to change the hymnody used in worship. Churches struggling with musical choices and styles of worship need this reminder: *Worship is about God, not us.* Whenever worship discussions become disoriented and begin with a list of preferences—my preferences versus your preferences—no one wins. There's no way out. A church cannot be all things to all people if preferences are the guide. Refocus the discussion on the One seated on the throne. Begin there. Then ask how your family of faith can best honor God and point others to him by means of the resources, people, and talents within your congregation. What is important is that personal preference not shape your worship, but that the use of the congregation's gifts shines the spotlight on God.

"I BELIEVE IN THE COMMUNION OF SAINTS"

If we gaze at John's picture in Revelation, we see gathered around the throne not just the current saints from the first century or just Christians of other past generations, but all Christians of every time and place. Leafing through God's family album, we see pictures of people from all tribes and nations and tongues, people of all different ages. Adults worship with kids. Christians from Cameroon join hands with Canadians. All are united around the throne. To have one exclusive musical voice dominate worship is not the picture of God's people. To use exclusively, say, music of the Baroque era, or of contemporary North American pop music, would not bind worshipers musically to Christians of every age and place.

Beyond the style of music used in worship, it's also important that the song texts used in worship relate to all aspects of the gospel message. In this picture of worship from Revelation, God's people *respond* to God—their response is their worship. This dialoguing (God acting, God's people responding) has happened all throughout the Bible, and it comes to a climax here. Worship is an authentic encounter with God, and these encounters result in emotions of lament (for sins committed against God and neighbor), of hope (for God's restorative work in our lives and in creation), and, yes, of praise (simply for who God is and for what he does). To focus singularly on any one of these aspects of worship would be to deny worshipers the totality of the Christian's story and to limit the dialogue to just one emotion.

In the following chapters I want to look at how each kind of church musician and worship leader can use his or her skill in the circle of praise and thus lead people to the throne of God in authentic worship.

QUESTIONS FOR REFLECTION AND DISCUSSION

1. Read Isaiah 6—the prophet's vision of heavenly worship. How does it compare and contrast with John's description in Revelation 4–5? Do you spot any similarities or differences?

2. Where is attention drawn during times of worship in your church? What gets in the way of members focusing on the triune God? What practical steps or remedies might help direct attention away from persons or things and toward God?

3. What is at the center of your church's worship? Is it God? Or is it an emphasis on teaching, evangelizing, entertaining, or soothing? Is that okay? Is there a way to do it all?

4. Does your worship limit the dialogue to one emotion? For example, are you predominantly singing praise songs *about* God, or *to* God? Or do you sing texts that are mostly about our sin and our need to make confession of sin? Review last week's song choices to see if you achieved a balance that relates to all the emotions of the Christian journey.

5. Beyond the music and music makers of a church, what else could be done to assemble people around God's throne more meaningfully? How could preachers, ushers, those who offer prayers or announcements, and other participants, as well as the visual environment and printed orders of worship, contribute to this sense? Share your ideas.

TWO

Planning for Worship

Father of Jesus, Love divine,
Great King upon your throne,
What joy to see you as you are
And worship you alone!
FREDERICK W. FABER

I'M DREAMING OF A SUNDAY WHEN . . .

As Jon and Joy pulled out of the garage, wondering again if they'd be late for church, their girls were crying because they had spilled orange juice all over their Sunday dresses. Jon lightened the moment by sharing his idea of the perfect Sunday. "Imagine a Sunday when everything goes right. The kids get dressed and make it through breakfast without spilling cereal on their clothes. You arrive at church twenty minutes early— plenty of time to spare. The preservice music draws you and other worshipers into the worship area. The call to worship is profound, yet brief, reminding you of the purpose of the hour. The opening song captures the joy and glory of God as worshipers lift their voices in song. The confession of sin and the assurance of God's pardon is real and freeing—it's as though the song about God's grace lifts tons of weight off people's shoulders. The Bible text for the sermon is read effectively. And the sermon—the sermon is a shot straight to the heart, biblically grounded and fresh, with relevant exegetical insights perfectly delivered with a variety of pace and inflection. No wonder the offering plates overflow and chairs have to be set up in the foyer for overflow seating." Jon would have continued, but they

21

were pulling into the church parking lot, ready to face the realities of a more mundane worship experience.

Does Jon's ideal Sunday sound like pie in the sky? Probably, at least with regard to worship on this side of eternity. But still, every once in a while, it wouldn't hurt worship leaders to reflect on the ideal—and then do the difficult and rewarding work of planning for it.

CHURCH LEADERS UNITE!

In the previous chapter we saw that worship exists to glorify God, the One seated on the throne. In worship we gather to bring our praise to God. Worship leaders direct worshipers' attention to God and facilitate this meeting between God and his people.

To ensure the quality of worship, many churches appoint a worship committee, worship planning committee, or an elder, deacon, or trustee whose responsibilities include worship oversight. Some churches may have full-time staff persons or ministers whose specific task is to coordinate and plan worship.

Whatever your own role may be, or however your church addresses the nurturing and massaging of your worship program, the mandate is the same for all: to nourish a healthy worship life that focuses attention on God.

To help you nourish and grow your worship program, here are some key support groups you may want to implement if you haven't already done so:

The Worship Board

The worship board is a group of persons—five or six for the average-sized church—who regularly meet together to discuss the worship life of the church. Their mandate is to facilitate worship that points to God, seeking to minimize any distractions that may be present during worship. As such, the worship board oversees nitty-gritty details: requesting budgeted funds in the annual church budget, lining up musicians for services, ordering poinsettias for the Christmas season, and so forth. Sadly, many worship boards stop there.

What if the worship board were to expand its influence to discuss all aspects of the worship experience?

The Worship Service Planners

A subset of people could be drawn from the membership of the worship board or from the congregation at large whose mandate is to plan specific worship services. The worship planners would meet on a regular basis with the pastor(s) to discuss upcoming sermon themes and Scripture texts. Beginning with this information, worship planners go to work. How can the call to worship this week introduce or highlight the sermon theme or Scripture text that is read later in the service? Or should the invitation to worship call attention to the season of the church year—Advent, Lent, and the like? Working with a theme gives unity, guidance, and overall shape to worship. Hymns, songs, and responsive readings all contribute to the theme. To this end, it's important that worship planners are prepared and come armed with many suggestions and that they familiarize themselves thoroughly with the multitude of resources available to worship planners—hymnbooks, worship journals, and denominational worship guides. In appendix 2, you will find a "Worship Planning Checklist" you may want to photocopy or adapt for use in your service planning.

Ideally, musicians would be invited to the worship planning meetings. Since they, along with the pastor(s), will have responsibility to lead the worship service, it's important that their input be included in shaping the service. Furthermore, after hearing the pastor preview the sermon, musicians who will lead the worship songs get a better idea of how to lead so that the songs fit stylistically with the sermon. For example, at the planning meeting the pastor discloses that next week's sermon will end with a powerful story of a person on his deathbed who gave testimony to God's grace even in the last breaths of life. The worship planners choose to conclude the service by singing "Amazing Grace." Had the musicians not been at the meeting, they might have assumed that the concluding song should be done in a grand and triumphant style. Now that they know the sermon's conclusion, however, the musicians reconsider how best to lead the hymn—perhaps in a quieter, more reflective style.

To that end, musicians can ask good questions of the pastor and worship planners: Can you summarize in one sentence what the sermon will be about? What response do you want to evoke in the congregation—trust, comfort, hope, resolve? What are some ways to involve more people in our worship this week?

As worship planners talk together, other insightful questions are asked: How can our instrumentalists and musicians better draw out the praise of the people? Are we singing too much hymnody or too many praise songs that don't challenge us intellectually? Or, on the other hand, do too many of our songs assume advanced theological awareness? Can we balance the two? One wise professor of church music once said that every church service should have "something old, something borrowed, and something blue." By this, she meant that the balance of a congregation's musical diet should be eclectic and include something from the church of the past ("something old"), something from the worldwide church ("something borrowed"), and something from the church of today ("something blue"). This formula works well to ensure that all God's people give voice to their worship of God in a well-rounded way.

After the worship planners form a rough sketch of the service, they communicate the plan to all who will be involved, as well as to those not-so-involved. Does the church custodian need to know of any change of schedule or set-up needs as a result of our plan for the worship service? Could the children sing this song in church school so that when they join us for worship they will know it? Could we create a children's bulletin to complement the worship theme of the day? Are there symbols from the Scripture text that we could place in our worship space—stones, wheat, vines, bread, and the like? Are there in-house artists who could be commissioned to produce works of art for us? In the church—as in most volunteer organizations—preplanning, overcommunicating, and broad involvement by all members are essential ingredients.

Worship planners pray. Even our best-laid plans are futile without God's blessing. So worship planners conclude their planning session by praying together, asking God to use the music and message, and all the elements of the service, to bring glory to God and to unite worshipers in their praise of God. Worship planners pray for the guest who may be present, asking that he or she would meet Jesus through worship. Worship planners pray for minimal distractions during worship, and they pray that worship leaders would become less so that God would become greater.

Worship planners arrive at worship on Sunday with a sense of anticipation. They communicate confidence to other planning team members and to all worship participants. They walk through the sanctuary doors with a spirit of thanksgiving. They sit in silence prior to the service, meditating on God—giving nonverbal cues to others that it's time to prepare for worship. They sing songs with enthusiasm. They fill the sanctuary with prayer and with praise of God. Their spirit of joy and thanksgiving is contagious.

At the next meeting, worship planners don't ask, "Did this work?" but, "What else could we do?" A synergy soon arises that gives the congregation's worship a unique shape and voice, because it is now worship *of* the congregation. And because planning and participation have been shared by many, ownership of and enthusiasm for worship are widespread within the congregation.

Through it all, worship planners remember that people's praise is at the heart of worship. They have done all they can do to invite people into the circle of praise around God's throne.

What a blessed and liberating moment it is when worship planners realize that God doesn't call their church to be just like somebody else's church. God uses different churches, with unique and various gifts and patterns of worship, to bring glory to him in different ways. Not all churches have to look alike; they don't need to model themselves after other "successful" churches. In fact, the reason these other churches are successful is that they have first discovered their unique gifts and have translated them into meaningful service within their community and within their community of faith.

Several excellent resources exist for worship planners.[1] Remember, the central question for all worship planners and music leaders is this: How can we, as organizers of this faith community's worship, better direct the worshipers' attention to God? Any other goal for worship planners will only result in an entertainment treadmill, where next week's service has to be a notch above last week's in order to keep the interest alive. That sort of worship planning is doomed, because *we* are at the center and not God. Remember, true worship naturally directs worshipers toward the One seated on the throne.

Every once in a while, worship planners would do well to step out of weekly worship planning and talk about the overall worship program—addressing larger questions and plans:

❏ How are our bulletins laid out? Are they clear and easy to follow? Is there enough white space, or do we cram too much information in too little space? Conversely, do we print too little information, unknowingly causing our guests to wonder about things and thus distract them from worship? (For instance, is it clear how we partake of the Lord's Supper? Who is welcome, who is not?) Do we use in-house lingo or abbreviations that would confuse a guest?

---

[1] Three "must have" resources: *Lift Up Your Hearts: Resources for Planning Worship* by Howard D. Vanderwell and Norma Dewaal Malefyt (Grand Rapids: CRC Publications [now Faith Alive Christian Resources] and New York: Reformed Church Press, 1995); *The New Handbook of the Christian Year* by Hoyt L. Hickman, Don E. Saliers, Laurence Hull Stookey, and James F. White (Nashville: Abingdon, 1992); and the quarterly journal *Reformed Worship* (Grand Rapids: Faith Alive Christian Resources), which includes balanced articles on worship planning, music ideas, and theology.

SERVING IN YOUR CHURCH MUSIC MINISTRY

❏ Will guests know where to find our nursery? Once they get there, are they welcomed by warm, caring, and trust-worthy people? If guests are at ease because they know their child will be well cared for during the worship hour, it's easier to focus attention on worship.

❏ Look at the overall flow of the worship service. Are there too many "commercials" by the pastor or other ministry leaders? Are there other ways to communicate announce-ments to the congregation?

❏ Visually, does our worship space define a "center"? What is the center of our worship? Is this reflected architec-turally? Is the Bible the center? The pulpit? The cross? A vase of flowers? A guitar stand?

❏ Is there too much clutter in our worship space? Could artists help us with such aspects as color and furniture placement to create a mood for gathering around the throne? Could our artistic members be invited to create new banners for the sanctuary or works of art that could be reproduced on the weekly worship folder?

❏ Who are the participants in our worship service? Is our worship reflective of all God's people—do we involve many, including persons from all age groups? Does one person, or a select group of people, "do" the worship while others simply watch? Or is our worship participa-tion too much of a good thing—so it seems like a parade of emcees doing a lot of disjointed exercises that fail to direct our attention to God?

❏ What kind of preparation do we give lay readers and worship participants? There are many excellent articles and resources that provide simple but important lessons for those who speak publicly. Could our church designate money in the budget for bringing in a communication professional to work with your cadre of Scripture readers? The Word of God read simply, clearly, and intelligently is powerful indeed!

❏ Are our greeters and ushers on board with the worship vision of our church?[2] Your church leaders may want to consider providing consistent yearly training for pivotal "behind the scenes" persons such as greeters (if your church doesn't yet have people who welcome members and guests, you might implement this volunteer position), ushers, and nursery workers. Oftentimes, these are the first people worshipers encounter. If one sees a warm and welcoming look on their faces, one will want to participate in worship with people such as these.

The Pastor

Pastors play a formative role in focusing the faith community's worship on God, both as a participant during the service of public worship and as a cheerleader for the musicians and worship planners. Pastors may be the most important part of the music program!

A good pastor understands and values worship. Just as worship focuses on God, so the life of the church revolves around worship. The sanctuary is the primary meeting place in the church building. Out of worship flow the music programs,

---

[2]Helpful resources include two other books in this Zondervan Practical Ministry Guide series—*Serving as a Church Greeter* and *Serving as a Church Usher.*

outreach programs, and education programs. With such a central focus to the life of the church, worship ought to be a very high priority for a pastor.

Some well-intentioned but misguided pastors confuse worship with "sermon," and sometimes even think good worship *is* (only) a good sermon. From there it's one small step to preparing only for the sermon and missing out on weekly opportunities to lead the congregation in other (non-sermon) acts of worship. Pastors need to understand and appreciate all the elements of the worship service.

When I was in college, I served on the campus worship planning committee. Students on the committee took turns as worship leaders and would call the preaching pastor for their particular week. I once placed such a call, introducing myself and sharing with the pastor what I would be doing in the service. I told him that I'd like all the components of worship to focus on the sermon theme, and then I asked if he had any input. His answer was unforgettable: "Oh, you just lead the preliminaries any way you want. Just make sure you leave me a good forty-five minutes for the sermon."

Insightful and effective pastors value the *entire* hour of worship, sensitive to how all acts of worship prepare hearts and minds to acknowledge and celebrate God and his mighty acts of love and grace. Pastors use carefully chosen words to invite people to worship, to draw them into the praise of God, and to elicit heartfelt confession of sin that leads to majestic praise for God's saving grace. To enable this important work, pastors keep worship as their central focus and set aside quality time not only for sermon planning but for service planning. Pastors reflect the importance of worship by the amount of budgeted dollars in the annual ministry plan they set aside for worship ministries; what's more, they show their commitment by giving consistent and positive feedback to worship participants.

Most of all, pastors reflect critically about their role in worship. Worship is about God; it must not be about the pastor. How can I as a pastor naturally point worshipers to God? Do I have an unhealthy need to be the center of attention? Is my sermon God-centered and based on Scripture? When pastors prepare well so that they avoid an embarrassing mediocrity, when they become true servants of God in public worship and give themselves to being conduits for God's Spirit, God is truly worshiped and magnified—when pastors become less, God becomes greater.

Worship boards, worship planners, and pastors live to bring worshipers before the throne of God.

But we have yet to discuss the vital work of church musicians—keyboardists, singers, and instrumentalists. How can they serve to direct attention not to themselves but to God? It is this important topic we take up in the next chapter.

QUESTIONS FOR REFLECTION AND DISCUSSION

1. So how are you doing? Does everyone in your faith community support and reflect the core values of your worship?

2. Do you value your worship enough to give your pastor(s) time and money for continuing worship education opportunities?

3. Could you plan a workshop for your worship leaders, lay readers, greeters, and ushers? Should you call in an expert, or could you plan and lead something yourselves? Brainstorm several options.

4. How is worship planning carried out in your church at present? Is it effective? Is there a way to involve more persons in worship planning?

5. Is your worship planning communication clear and thorough? How can you best coordinate your efforts as church school teachers, artists, youth group leaders, worship leaders, pastors, instrumentalists, keyboardists, singers?

THREE

Serving at the Keyboard

God,
help me to take a moment
as I sit here before
the ebony and ivory.
As I adjust the bench,
may I be adjusted as well.
Help me to make the transition,
now,
from playing the notes correctly,
to praying the music
more completely.

DAVID HAAS

WORTHY IS CHRIST!

Of all the meaningful acts of worship, perhaps none is more appreciated than that which is performed by good leaders of congregational singing. With a sensitive pianist, the congregation gains confidence to sing heartily. With an inspiring organist who uses color, variety, and the full resources of the instrument, sung text is encountered and offered in a new way. The congregation values keyboardists who breathe new life into the songs of the congregation.

Recall the scene from Revelation 4–5 where God's creation did not merely gather, as though the point were a mere assemblage of God's creatures. No, the cosmos gathered around God *in order to worship.* They gathered to respond to the sight of the

One seated on the throne and to remember the work of the Lamb. And part of that response took the shape of a hymn, words sung to music with the voice. They sang "Holy, holy, holy . . ." and "You are worthy . . ." and "You are worthy . . ." (again) and "Worthy is the Lamb . . ." and "To him who sits on the throne and to the Lamb. . . ." The five songs share a common theme, for each is about the worthiness (literally the "worth-ship"—the origin of the English word *worship*) of God. All living creatures in heaven and on earth gathered *to sing* of the worth-ship of Jesus Christ. I wonder what their music sounded like!

If the primary purpose of worship is to gather around the throne, the primary function of the musician must be to enable people to sing their songs of praise as they gather around God's throne. Sadly, church musicians sometimes lose sight of this fundamental aspect of their work.

SURVEY SAYS . . .

A survey conducted by a musical organization asked church musicians how they spent their time preparing for worship. At the same time, the surveyors asked congregations what they valued most from their church musicians—that is, in what area did they want their musicians to spend time preparing for worship? The results were surprising. (Well, maybe not.) Church musicians responded (overwhelmingly) that they spent their time rehearsing service music. Organists worked hard at fingering preludes and fugues. Keyboardists practiced bravura piano études that sent their hands ducking and weaving.

Guitarists worked out their fingerings for solos. Alarmingly, the survey showed that most church musicians gave little time to the songs the congregation was to sing, except perhaps for a "once through" just before the service.

The congregations' responses revealed quite a different need. Congregations said that, while they enjoy good service music, what they value most are sensitive and energizing accompaniments to their songs. They desire musicians who are in tune with their particular congregation's voice and who accompany songs with thought, creativity, and skill. Congregations want to sing well!

This is not to say that preludes, offertories, and postludes are not important. Surely they are. It is simply to remind church musicians that their primary focus is enabling and energizing the song of the people.

God's people gather to sing.

BACK TO THE BASICS: MUSICAL TRUST OR BUST

For a congregation to sing well, it must first know that it can musically trust the song accompanist—be it organist, electronic keyboardist, or pianist. Knowingly or unknowingly, musicians build trust by their mastery of basic technical skills at the keyboard. A steady tempo, clean articulation on attacks and releases, pauses for breaths, introductions that are helpful and clear—executed well and consistently, these are all musical techniques a musician uses to earn a congregation's trust.

Put another way, if I, a singer, am going to sing enthusiastically, I need to know when the musician intends for me to begin singing. Otherwise I'll tend to wait until everyone else has begun—and only then will I feel safe in joining my voice with theirs. However, when the musician is unmistakably clear about how long he or she will hold (or not hold) the last note of a stanza, when I'm certain that the introduction is completed and it's time for me to sing, then I can join in full voice because I consciously—or, most often, unconsciously—trust the musical leadership of the musician. An insecure congregation is a hesitant one, but a secure congregation sings with gusto.

Musicians, if you're still unclear about this point, try this easy experiment at your next worship service. Listen—carefully listen—to how many voices are singing on the exact downbeat of each stanza of a particular song. Don't sing along yourself; just listen. In most congregations, it isn't until a few beats later that all the voices are singing and thus creating a small crescendo at the beginning of each new stanza.

If this describes what's happening in your song leadership, try this. In your preparation for worship, think about how much space (rest) the congregation will need between the verses of a song. Can you make it consistent? How can you give a clear break between the stanzas?

One simple technique to consider: Write in your music the amount of time you will hold the song's last note (1–2–3, for example), and how much time you will rest (= R). Thus: 1–2–3-R–R, and on the first R lift your hands to stop the sound. Use this formula as you play the introduction to the song. Be consistent. Without even realizing it, the congregation will implicitly understand when to end and when to begin, and without fail they'll be with you on the downbeat of the next stanza. You've gained their trust. They will relax and sing more confidently.

Now take the opportunity to listen again. The results will amaze you! And it's just the beginning step on your way to facilitating better congregational singing.

MORE MUSICAL TRUST

Master other basics so that poor technique does not become a point of distraction. Remember that we want to *help* in all we do, not hinder the song of the people. Organists, drill the pedal line alone so that it's not merely a thumping drone underneath the manuals. Pianists, be careful not to overplay the piano. Keyboardists, are you using only tempo for effect? All keyboardists have a variety of techniques at their disposal: be sure to learn them. Practice them. Use them well.

Think about the tempo needed for each song. Musical questions that guide the decision regarding tempo might be, How fast can I think the thoughts of the text? Is the music simple, or more complex? Is this an old favorite of the congregation, or a tune that will take some time to learn? Nonmusical questions are also important—What is the acoustic like in the room? What is the size of my congregation? What time of day is the service—early morning (oh, no!), afternoon, evening? The answers to all these questions will combine to guide tempo choice. But once a musician establishes the tempo, be sure to lead! Left to itself, the congregation will naturally drag down the tempo. They need a musical leader to keep them on track. They need you!

Again, here's the big idea: By not calling attention to either a self-conscious virtuosity or an embarrassing mediocrity, keyboardists *enable the people to sing.* They bring much preparation and thought to the leading of each song. To enable people to sing well, musicians have to be in tune with what they can do to support singers. Encouraging the song of the people is our main job.

GOD IS IN THE DETAILS

After working out technique, we turn our attention to understanding the placement of each particular song within the worship service, asking how each song functions in worship.

Begin by studying each song away from the worship space, and even away from a keyboard. Sing the song through in your mind. With your inner ear try different tempi, harmonization, and instrumentation. Let yourself go! I find that for me this is best done early in the morning when I'm still lying in bed; it's a pleasant way to begin the day—an imaginary orchestra playing through Sunday's songs in my head!

Then research the author and composer of the text and music. What was the intended purpose for the song, the occasion for its writing? Where and how will this song be used in worship—an opening song of praise, a prayerful response to the sermon, a prayer of confession?

Next, move on to musical questions. What is the musical language of the song—contemporary, Caribbean, Baroque, Genevan psalm tune, or something else? Is this song an old friend of the congregation, or a new guest I need to introduce? Are there previously published resources for this tune I could use, or should I create my own opus from scratch?

Now that you've moved into this stage of the process, begin thinking within the parameters of the musical style. Songs come off best when they are treated honestly. Baroque and

Victorian hymns work well on the organ; Caribbean folk tunes need percussive instruments and a wash of different musical textures; radio gospel hymns work well on the piano; jazz idioms prefer piano and string bass. I'm not saying that a gospel hymn can never be played on the organ or that an electronic keyboard can never play Caribbean music. I'm simply observing that the style of the song is who it is. Try to make the most of it, not the least of it. Bring out the song's personality and let it shine as it was intended.

Then put it all together: "The opening song this Sunday is a Genevan psalm tune and the text is about the greatness of God. The congregation has sung the tune before—but it may sound new to some."

That done, go again to the keyboard and get to work. In this example, an opening hymn about the greatness of God suggests strength and boldness, so the people should sing with full voice and with full confidence that *their God is great!* Begin with a solid introduction to the song. Work to replicate the desired effect you heard in your head when you were thinking of the song as you spent time away from the keyboard. Did you hear full sounds and rich harmony that reflected the text about God's greatness in creation? Vary the sound and interpretation of each stanza to fit the message of the text. Be creative! In this instance a Genevan psalm tune could be played triumphantly on an organ but also very effectively with a small Renaissance ensemble of, say, clarinets and violins with a tambourine.

Listen now to how your congregation responds to your thought, preparation, and musical leadership!

Keyboardists who wish to expand their technique to include different musical styles could challenge themselves to try some self-tutorials.[3] Many excellent resources and Web sites exist that teach different styles. Perhaps part of each week's rehearsal could be devoted to studying and understanding different genres. Exercises could be used to build more accurate interpretations of each particular style. Expanding musical horizons is a good thing! Many keyboardists have skills in classical and Baroque genres, but today's well-rounded musician also needs to be exposed to global music, gospel music, and the like. Self-tutorials are effective, fun ways to keep musical skills sharp.

ORGANISTS

The pipe organ is one of the finest worship instruments ever created. As a wind instrument, it naturally supports the human voice—another wind instrument. Understand the stops, the pitches, and the capabilities and limitations of the organ you use. Use its sounds and colors and textures to enable your members to sing their best.

One organist I know sits down once a year at the organ he plays and purposely does *not* practice. Rather, he uses this time to methodically play each stop alone, one at a time. He plays certain stops up an octave, plays others down an octave. He lis-

---

[3]For Spanish music, I recommend studying the appendices of *Libro de Liturgia y Cántico* (Minneapolis: Augsburg Fortress, 1998), which in addition to tips on instrumentation and style includes a wonderful resource of Spanish rhythm patterns. For gospel music, see *Praise Him with the Gospel!* by Charles F. Little, who meticulously handwrote gospel accompaniments for many familiar hymns (Milwaukee, Wis.: Dove Music). For improvisation and global music, see David Cherwien's *Let All the People Sing: A Keyboardist's Creative and Practical Guide to Engaging God's People in Meaningful Song* (St. Louis, Mo.: Concordia, 1997).

tens carefully. Then he goes on to the next stop with the same routine—playing chords with this stop drawn, playing a solo melody line, listening some more. Then he tries new combinations of sounds with stops he's never tried together before. He says it never ceases to amaze him how he finds new color and new sounds from an instrument he thought he had musically exhausted.

Try this exercise with *your* instrument. Throw caution to the wind and be courageous. Use new sound combinations in worship. Are you singing Psalm 23—the verse about walking through the valley of the shadow of death? Perhaps this is the time to create a dark sound that contrasts with the warm sounds of the opening verses. Is the song one that speaks of our need to confess our sins to God? Perhaps a clear, simple sound would be best. Could a solo or accompanied trumpet stop herald the opening hymn on Easter morning? For a gospel hymn, try using only a 4' flute for the introduction (think "calliope"). Or for hymn tunes from, say, the time of the Renaissance, try playing the chorale with a more "open" touch using an 8' krummhorn. Or another time try a 2' solo as a hymn introduction! Be creative!

Understand—and love—the instrument you play. Use it to its fullest capacity. Understand the song you are leading, and let that understanding guide interpretation. Engage yourself in the song of the people, and they will sing like they've never sung before. Use your creativity to bring hymns to life in a new way, and the congregation will sing their songs of praise with renewed energy. But in order for this to happen, organists—and all keyboardists, for that matter—must give priority to song leading in their weekly preparation!

PIANISTS

Pianists face a greater challenge than organists, for the piano has one sound and one timbre. Variation cannot come from adding or subtracting stops, and changes in volume result from how firmly or gently one plays into the keys. Therefore, pianists need to work extra hard on their attacks and releases and take care to use consistent tempo. Also, because of the percussive nature of the instrument, pianists must resist the urge to over-play the piano. Let the piano's tone speak naturally and unforced into the room.

That said, it is possible to have the piano sing with different voices. Try playing up an octave; try soloing out the melody with the left hand, an octave lower; vary the touch from staccato to legato phrasing; try using arpeggios—imagine you're playing a harp or guitar, and listen to what happens! If the piano is the primary accompaniment instrument for a congregation, the pianist may want to double the bass voice in octaves while playing the other three voices with the right hand.

Like organists, pianists must give priority to song leading in their weekly preparation.

KEYBOARDISTS

Churches have seen an explosive rise in the use of electronic keyboards. Electronic keyboards provide an amazing variety of sound and speak clearly into even the largest of rooms. They are generally less expensive than a grand piano and certainly less costly than a pipe organ.

The danger here, again, is that electronic keyboards—like organs and pianos—can easily direct attention to the players rather than point people toward God. If you use the solo electronic keyboard to lead singing, be judicious in the sound you select. The best thing you can do to effectively lead the congregation is to play clearly, with consistent tempo and phrasing, and to choose sounds that support the singing while not overwhelming it. On the other hand, if you are accompanying the congregation with the electronic keyboard as part of an ensemble, then your role is different. Support the other instruments well, and be sure to select appropriate sounds in order to add to the texture.

And, once again, prioritize song leading in your weekly preparation! Your congregation will love you for it.

PRAYING TWICE

An early church leader named Augustine once said, "To sing well is to pray twice." Meaningful text is one thing, but to set it to a great tune that gives the text new life when it is sung—that indeed is to pray twice.

Congregations want to sing well and thereby to pray twice. They need musicians who understand what it is they are doing and what it is they have been called to do. So learn to use your instrument well—whether it's a squeaky upright piano or a new million-dollar pipe organ. Enable your congregation to sing more powerfully their songs of praise to the One seated on the throne.

QUESTIONS FOR REFLECTION AND DISCUSSION

1. Is the song of the people the main emphasis in your worship music? If not, what is?

2. How could your congregation learn to sing better?

3. John Calvin, the great Reformer, once said that "all church music is really sung prayer." Do you agree or disagree? Tell why.

4. Is your church's physical environment and the placement of your instruments conducive to good singing?

5. Talk through the opening song for your next worship service. Answer the following questions to help you think of ways to bring this song to life:

   • From what nation is its origin?

   • What does it say to us and to God?

   • What's the meter and key?

   • How well do our people know this tune?

   • How could we sing this in a new way?

   • Will it need a lengthy introduction, or a brief one?

- In a perfect setting (no-holds-barred!), how would this song be done? What might be preventing us from doing it that way?

6. What educational opportunities exist in your area where your musicians could recharge their batteries? (I'm not thinking of a music performance school but rather of workshop leaders, clinicians, and teachers who understand and promote congregational singing as the church musician's chief priority.)

FOUR

Serving with Your Voice

Father, grant that what we sing with our lips
We may believe in our hearts.
And what we believe in our hearts
May we show forth in our lives.
Through Jesus Christ our Lord. Amen.

FROM AN ENGLISH BOOK OF PRAYERS, LATE 1800s

THE CENTER OF PRAISE: OUR SONG

Our frank and loving friends Jon and Joy enjoy a new appreciation for the skills and thought of their worship keyboardist, which allows them to focus on God. They look forward to Wednesday evening choir rehearsals because the choir director is energetic and creative, while also musically gifted and spiritually sensitive about the choir's work. They have a note posted on their refrigerator, reminding them of the profound words of Charles Wesley: "The word of God touched me, but the music moved me." Because of the new vision of their church's worship program, Jon and Joy are reenergized and immersed in the music programs.

Indeed, the unique activity of the church—namely, the worship of God—is energized by song.[4] Our sung praise in worship is our response to God's action. Whether a choir, ensemble, praise team, or congregation, the church gathers groups of singers to assist her in worship. Isn't it wonderful that

---

[4]Anyone not convinced on this point could read John L. Bell's *The Singing Thing* (Chicago: GIA Publications, G-1550), a handbook that explores the reason we humans are compelled to express ourselves in song.

we are hard-pressed to find a church today that does *not* have singers assisting in worship? It only makes sense, for we were made to worship, and we were made to sing.

Like keyboard musicians (see the last chapter), singers serve to focus worshipers' attention on God, not on themselves. Let's now examine how singers can serve vocally in leading God-directed worship.

THE CHOIR

The main purpose of the modern choir is to assist the congregation in worship. Before the reformation of the church in the 1600s, choirs were exclusively male and comprised only of clergy—monks and priests. Pre-Reformation choirs worshiped on the people's behalf, while the laity observed worship from behind closed iron gates leading to the nave of the church. After the Reformation, Protestant churches eliminated clergy choirs in an effort to give worship back to the people, while Vatican councils later made similar recommendations to Roman Catholic churches. Where choirs were reestablished, it was clear that they were not to "do worship" on behalf of the congregation; rather, they were to assist the congregation in singing their songs with renewed energy.

The Choir's Involvement in Worship

Choirs can lead worship in many different and equally effective ways:

1. Choirs enliven congregational song by singing a single stanza of a particular hymn or song. Many times hymns

or songs have several stanzas, each reflecting a different mood or idea. The choir singing in alternation with the congregation serves not only to interpret different ideas present in the text but also to give the congregation vocal rest during an otherwise lengthy song.

2. The choir can sing a descant (an alternate melody above the tune) on selected songs. This doesn't need to be limited to sopranos, though it is the voice typically chosen for such a part. Having the tenors join the descant (an octave lower) gives the sopranos additional support. Descants can be found in many published hymnbooks and leader's guides, or inventive choir directors can write descants of their own to fit a particular hymn and occasion.

3. Many hymns and songs lend themselves to canonical singing—that is, the melody can be sung behind itself (much like a round). Choirs can sing the canon, following the congregation. Singing in canon is another musical way to illumine a text or to render a familiar song in a new way. If your congregation is not accustomed to singing in canon, you might begin by using the final stanza of "Amazing Grace." The text focuses on eternity ("When we've been there ten thousand years"), so use the choir in canon to create the sense of a thousand voices singing in perpetuity. Indicate by verbal announcement or in the worship folder that the last stanza is to be sung in canon—the congregation will begin, and the choir will join two measures later.

4. The choir can offer a hymn concertato (a hymn-based anthem inviting the participation of both congregation and choir). The choir can rehearse its part, and clear

instructions can be given during worship as to when the congregation should join in the singing. Concertatos are especially useful and effective because typically they use instrumentation and varying harmonies not found in hymnbooks. Here is an opportunity to use instrumentalists from the congregation, should the score ask for them.

5. The choir can serve as group cantor, or soloist. The choir can sing the psalm, or it can lead in a sung response to Scripture or to other elements in the service. Choir directors can use a choir rehearsal to do a dry run of the week's upcoming service, singing through some or all of the service music. On Sunday, then, the choir serves as a group of singers who have already familiarized themselves with some of the service music, which can be a great benefit to the congregation.

6. When the congregation is learning a new song, the choir can assist by singing the song through first. This allows the congregation to more quickly focus on the text and removes some of the apprehension that accompanies an unknown tune. When the congregation does begin to sing, the choir continues to provide strong vocal support.

7. The choir can offer an anthem (a musical work written for choir alone). Too often this is the only way choirs participate in worship in most churches. As the choir sings the anthem, the congregation is asked to participate, not with voice, but with mind. The idea is that the choir offers a piece of music on the congregation's behalf.

Let me add a couple of notes about the anthem:

❏ If the congregation is asked to worship by means of the choir anthem, then it is important that the congregation knows and understands the text the choir is singing. Choir directors can insist on clear diction and uniform vowels. Worship planners and bulletin editors can see to it that a copy of the text appears in the worship folder or on an overhead screen.

❏ The anthem does not always have to be in the "anthem slot." Rest assured, no "worship police" stand by, ready to arrest a church that moves the anthem out of the regular slot! Look at the text of the anthem: What does it say? Is it a call to confession? Then use it as such. Does it thematically tie in with the Scripture passage? Then use it as a response to the Scripture reading. Does it complement the sermon? Then use it as a prayer response to the sermon. Does the text ask others to join in the praise of God? Then use it as the call to worship. Use your choir anthem to assist in the flow of worship and to direct people's attention to God—whenever and however it can best do so.

The Choir Member

Choir members function best when they understand that, above all, they are part of a team. As team players, they show up! They prioritize choir rehearsals as a commitment, and even let this commitment override emotions of the day ("I'm tired"; "I don't feel like it"). They concentrate on the music and on the instruction of the director. They have a sharp pencil in their choir folders—and use it constantly! While choir members listen and carefully watch the director, they know that they are really singing for God and that singing—the "sacrifice of praise"—is leading God's people in worship. They know that their participation in the choir is a holy calling, and they thrill to being part of something unifying and beautiful within the church.

The Choir Director

The choir director is equal parts musician, accountant, cheerleader, minister, masseuse, and counselor. Rarely does a job in the church expect so much from one person, and rarely does the church receive so much from one person. Choir directors are beacons of hope who never let singers settle into mediocrity. They give them repertoire and musical experiences to grow into, not out of.

A choir director naturally understands his or her role as the leader of a group of singers who make music. Music is not a god unto itself but exists in the church to point people to God—the One seated on the throne. A choir director understands this—so choir directors go about their work with this intentional purpose and in the process discover a holy, fun, and musical calling.

Choir directors prepare well. Before the singers arrive—months before—the choir director is busy. When singers arrive at the first rehearsal, there are no distractions that will waste time or cause frustration. The music is there—purchased (not photocopied!), three-hole punched (if that's how your singers store music in their folders), stamped with the church's name (for all those pieces of music that seem to walk out of the music room), and plentiful in number (to avoid the "but I don't have that one!" cries during rehearsal). Inside the folder is a printed worship and choir schedule. Singers know the Sundays they will sing and mark their calendars (or PDAs) accordingly. When the director anticipates these things, distractions can be removed from the rehearsal. (Perhaps a volunteer could be recruited from the choir to assist in some of the logistical details and the folder and music preparation.)

Choir directors work with other church and choir leaders so that choir rehearsals are easy to attend. Would having a nursery allow more singers to join the choir? Is another evening or another time slot more convenient for all members? Is the rehearsal space roomy and conducive to singing? Choir members will soon learn by your attention to detail that you consider the music program significant and their participation in it crucial.

Choir directors provide balanced repertoire that is new, old, interesting, challenging, and simple! Know your choir's skill, and then push them within those limits with certain selections, while rewarding them with well-known favorites. Stylistically, repertoire should be balanced by the use of the best of all eras of church music.

Singers come to sing, not to sit through a lecture or to be bothered with shortages of music or with unclear demands. Let singers sing! Help them sing well. Some choir directors lead rehearsals where there is more talking than singing. Instead of using words of correction, try modeling by singing the line correctly and musically; to do so can often communicate more clearly than obscure remarks such as, "I need more legato there."

Choir directors pace the rehearsal so that it is energizing and rewarding. Start with physical warm-ups that release physical tension (back rubs, loosening-up exercises, a moment of silence, lying down on the pews). Slowly introduce vocalises into the warm-up. Listen for tension in the sound, and relax the tension through more loosening-up exercises. Aim for a free flow of the voice unencumbered by fatigue or physical tension in the neck, back, and larynx. Begin rehearsal with a hymn or song preview for Sunday's worship—and insist on singing it with as much energy and interest as you would expect from an anthem. Then vary the rehearsal repertoire with selections that move from difficult to easy, from major to minor; end with something that is a guaranteed success.

Choir directors weigh their words carefully. Like all volunteers, choir members respond when they are verbally pulled, not pushed. Speak clearly, slowly, and with an economy of verbiage. Remember that every comment is an indirect suggestion. Use communal language to reinforce the reality that a choir is a team ("We can do more with the commas on page 4," not "I wanted you to observe the commas on page 4—and you didn't!"). Use suggestion rather than command ("What would happen if we shaped the phrases around the word "holy" on the first page?" not "Sing it like it's printed!"). Be sure to negate the negative, and give praise every chance you get ("Can we have a softer sound from the sopranos here—just like you sang it so beautifully on page 2?" not "You're singing too loudly again!"). Use the passive voice ("The organ could play more loudly on the last chord," not, "Anita, shouldn't you pull out another stop there?") Like it or not, singers form perceptions of the choir director based on and shaped by the words used and the experiences shared with that person in rehearsal.

Working with pastors and worship boards or committees in the church's overall worship program, choir directors are specifically in tune with that week's worship service. They plan ahead. Where will the anthems best fit? Can we be creative with the placement of the choir this week (a call to worship that echoes from the balcony; a response to God's blessing that resounds from the fellowship hall)? Then—and this is key—choir directors think through the plan and communicate it clearly to the choir.

Sometimes the choir director uses creative communication to save the choir from a list of verbal reminders. Directors might publish a monthly one-page "Choir Chatter" newsletter that touches base and includes logistical and schedule reminders—and also contains a list of choir members' birthdays. They consider an e-mail newsletter for choir members. During especially hectic holiday times, maybe they distribute a "what you need to know for this Sunday" sheet in order to preserve valuable rehearsal time.

Choir directors come to rehearsal prepared for anything. Oftentimes our ideal plans must be laid aside, given the reality of certain situations. How well can we improvise? What's in our arsenal of musical techniques that will help us handle the musical train wrecks that knock us off balance? These "tricks in the hat" are picked up by observing other directors, attending conferences, or participating in another choir as a singer.

Choir directors model effective worship leadership. They remain calm, they guide, they facilitate worship. They arrive early, they anticipate questions and concerns, they check in with other worship leaders and gather the choir and prepare them for worship.

Cheerleading is part of a choir director's job description as well. After worship, the choir director has honest and edifying comments to share: "Altos—you were so 'on' today!" "Brent, I loved the organ introduction—it made that hymn sing with new life for me!" "Pastor Beem, thanks for letting us put the anthem after your sermon this week. I thought it really fit well there, didn't you?"

Choir directors give members time off. In today's fast-paced world, a night at home is a gift. Be sure to give this gift on occasion. When planning a semester's schedule, call the local school district to find out when spring break will be held—or winter break (usually in February)—and see if there are any three-day weekends scheduled. Perhaps one of those would be a Sunday you'll give the choir a break or not hold a rehearsal that week. Another idea: Give the men a week off and work only with sopranos and altos, and switch the next week. Consider "seasonal choirs" that gather only for a particular service or season, say, Christmas or Easter. Maybe even consider recruiting a "choir for a day."

Choir directors share their expertise beyond the choir. Insightful choir directors use church publications to write about the work of the choir. They write about worship. They coordinate a monthly column in the church newsletter to increase awareness of the choir's activities and its significance in the life of the church. Perhaps they even put a short paragraph in the weekly bulletin about the anthem being sung or about the history of a song. Choir directors use 1 Corinthians 14:15b as their theme verse: "I will sing with my spirit, but I will also sing with my mind."

Finally, choir directors watch an intimate small group grow right in front of them. Choir members will relish not only times of making music together, but they'll want times of fellowship as well. People will want Christmas parties, year-end parties, and kick-off potlucks. As choir members come together socially, they'll also bond musically as a team. Choir directors facilitate this social aspect of choir and even encourage it. When a member is ill or experiences a significant life event, cards are passed around and signed during rehearsal. When a member is absent, the director notices and places a personal call or sends an e-mail message to say that he or she was missed. The choir director takes an interest in each singer's life as a person and shares with him or her in the journey.

Through careful planning, along with realistic assessment of the strengths of a particular church and choir, the choir director leads the choir—and ultimately the congregation—in meaningful times of worship.

The Choir as Outreach Tool

Beyond the weekly worship participation, several other opportunities exist for choirs to be used as outreach tools for the church.

First, consider doing advertising in the community to recruit new choir volunteers. Many local newspapers will run religious ads for free. Many persons are seeking musical experiences, so why not invite them to a church choir—church member or not? All it takes is a simple paragraph in a newspaper, such as "This Wednesday the choir of Community Church begins its season of meaningful music and memorable fellowship! Won't you consider joining us? No audition is necessary, and there is

no cost. Join us at 7:00 P.M., and we'll be glad to meet you!" End
your notice with simple directions to the church, and include a
phone number or an e-mail address. You may be surprised at
how many people want to join your choir!

Here's another outreach idea: Plan a year-end festival worship service. This is the one service where all the choirs and
musicians pull off a "no-holds-barred" worship service heavily
advertised in the community. Perhaps the choir can learn a
magnum opus work from the choral repertoire.[5] Service planners
can develop a theme and then balance the rest of the service
with other anthems and songs. Plan for lots of congregational
participation—hymn concertatos, songs, and responsive readings. Use various instruments to accompany the choir and congregational singing—perhaps a small string quartet, brass,
handbells, or a full-size orchestra (maybe even all of these!).

In one church I served, we concluded each choir season
with such an event. We even invited a guest conductor to lead
the choirs. I began preparing the choirs months beforehand,
and the guest conductor then took the choirs to new levels of
finesse—plus I could relax and enjoy singing with my choir
once the guest conductor took over. Working on a *magnum
opus* piece of choral repertoire strengthened the choir and put

---

[5]By *magnum opus* works, I mean such works as Handel's *Messiah* (in
entirety, or doing individual parts); Robert Ray's *Gospel Mass*; Handel's *Coro-
nation Anthems*; Mendelssohn's *Hear My Prayer*; Gabriel Fauré's or John Rut-
ter's *Requiem*; Mozart's *Solemn Vespers*; John Ferguson's *Passion of St. John*; or
Randall Thompson's *Psalm of Thanksgiving*—just to name a few. Each of
these high-quality works is satisfying to sing, has a variety of instrumentation options, and is doable for the average choir. Each also presents an obvious theme that could be complemented by hymns and other brief and
simple anthems.

quality literature into the music files, while challenging the choir with a worthy goal.

Ask choir members and congregation members to invite family, friends, colleagues, and neighbors to this special worship service. Ask the evangelism committee to produce brochures and mail them to the community, and then to be present that evening to greet guests. Design posters, and ask choir members to distribute and post them at work, at neighborhood grocery stores, or at local coffeehouses. Send publicity notices to local newspapers, community calendars, community cable stations, and radio stations. Plan to have a social hour after the service.

To balance the year-end festivities, perhaps the choir could take the lead in a special worship service halfway through the church year—perhaps in December. This could take many shapes: a service of nine lessons and carols, a Christmas Eve candlelight worship service, or maybe even a choir caroling night that would take the place of a rehearsal.

The choir will not only feel good about working together to achieve a great musical accomplishment on such projects, but they'll also feel delighted to serve the church in drawing new people into the congregation.

THE PRAISE TEAM

The praise team is really a small(er) choir with a different name. The purpose is the same: to enable the congregation to sing their songs of praise to God. Thus, a praise team can benefit from the same list of ideas as the choir to fulfill its role in providing musical leadership for the congregation.

However, because the praise team evolved out of the "performance" emphasis of a rock band, there are more obstacles to overcome on the road to success (*success* being defined as "assisting and enabling the people to sing for themselves").

Praise teams usually contain fewer members than choirs do, and more often than not, the team selects its singers from the congregation—but it's crucial to move beyond any exclusivism in establishing the group. Like the choir, the praise team's membership should be open to all. This is not an elite group; it is a group whose purpose is to help the congregation better sing her songs of praise.

To enhance its opportunities for success, a praise team should carefully consider its positioning within the worship space, for logistical placement is crucial. A praise team's job is not to sing *at* the people or *for* the people; it is to sing *with* the people. Personally, I like to see the praise team stand in the same place as would a choir—in an area that allows them to lead but also to assist and support the congregation's voice. If the praise team needs to be amplified (and it may not need to be), be sure that its volume does not overwhelm the congregation's sound.

Many praise teams prefer to use texts projected on a wall or screen rather than hymnals. The goal is to get worshipers to look up, and, indeed, the congregation's singing is often improved tonally by this upward-oriented posture. However, consider these concerns: Is the text large enough to accommodate worshipers with poorer eyesight? Are we unknowingly limiting worship for the aged, those with visual impairments, or those seated in an area with poor sight lines?

Think about this question regarding projecting only text— with no musical notation: Are we limiting participation to only those who happen to know that particular tune? Would guests in your congregation be able to sing with full voice if they don't know the tune and don't have music to guide them?

Like the choir, the praise team is not an end unto itself. The praise team exists to enable the congregation to better sing her songs of praise.

THE SOLOIST

The church soloist is a one-person choir. The solo presentation of music boasts a long heritage in the Bible. Miriam, Deborah, Daniel, David, Mary, and Simeon were all soloists. Later in the church, chants required a soloist to sing the text, while the congregation sang a refrain—the same "call and response" form echoed in modern-day spirituals.

The soloist aids worship in much the same way as a choir or praise team. He or she can sing selected song stanzas, offer a sung prayer, sing responses throughout the service, help teach the congregation new tunes, and offer an anthem written for one voice only. Of course, the goal should never be to interrupt the worship by having soloists sing "special music"—random selections that have nothing to do with worship or the service theme but simply call attention to the singer.

Like the choir, the soloist can be used creatively and effectively in the worship service. Logistically, a soloist can easily be placed anywhere in the worship space. Some worshipers will appreciate a soloist who sings out of the congregation's view, allowing the congregation to focus more on the text than on the singer. For worshipers who are not accustomed to seeing the choir, placing the soloist in front might be beneficial, because worshipers will not only hear the words but also see the singer's posture and facial expressions. Discern the needs of your congregation and study the song, and then determine where the best placement would be.

Appropriate repertoire selection is crucial for the soloist:

❑ Did the soloist select a piece of music that falls naturally into his or her voice range?
❑ Is the piece of music well chosen for this particular congregation?
❑ Can our accompanist handle the music, or is it too difficult to play well?

The soloist—the one-person choir—has lots of sources from which to select music for worship. Sometimes singing directly from the congregation's hymnal is the simplest and the best thing to do. There are also many volumes of collected songs. Be sure to buy two copies—one for the soloist and one for the accompanist. Soloists can also look at larger vocal works, such as Handel's *Messiah* or Haydn's *The Creation*, and excerpt solos or arias.

THE CHILDREN'S CHOIR

Jesus urged little children to come to him. No wonder, for children are energetic, loving, open, and eager to participate (well, most of the time). Their simple faith is a winsome model for adults. When Isaiah and Zechariah describe the way they see heaven, both note the presence of children: Isaiah sees children playing near the holes of cobras in a perfect land of peace (11:8), and Zechariah notes that children are playing in the streets of the new city (8:5). Heavenly worship will certainly include the inquisitiveness, freshness, and vitality of youth.

It makes sense, then, to involve children in the heart of earthly worship. Far too often, children are talked down to in worship, used as cute props, or, worse yet, totally ignored.

Many churches harness the energy of children and involve them in worship as a children's choir (variously called Junior Choir, Children's Choir, Sunday School Singers, and so forth). Whatever you call this group of singers, a good children's choir director embodies all the things described in this chapter under the heading "The Choir Director"—and more. In addition to being able to run an effective rehearsal, in addition to being organized, thoughtful, theological, and communicative, in addition to having the patience of Job, the children's choir director also needs an accurate understanding of the child's developing voice *and* the ability to communicate this awareness effectively to children, using age-appropriate language.

Children's choir directors understand that many children have not been taught how to use their singing voices in a healthy way. Schoolteachers have spoken to them about an "inside voice" and an "outside voice." Parents have asked them to whisper during church. They've been asked by well-meaning volunteers at church school to "sing louder so Jesus can hear you." But few children have learned to experience their singing voices in a healthy manner.

Like all things in life, they need to be taught, so children's choir directors find creative ways to communicate and to model a healthy singing voice to children. They make sure that the music is not pitched too low. One way to enable children to sing brighter and better is to get them to focus on their "head tone"; music that is pitched correctly enables them to do so more naturally. Children's choir directors use object lessons to teach children in concrete and visual ways: a helium balloon on a string shows children how to hold their heads high but not tight; throwing an imaginary baseball while the choir sings a certain phrase gets them to project sound. Children's choir directors focus on vocal production, uniformity of vowels, breath support—good singing skills that will serve the singers their entire lives.

Most songs should be done in unison. Perhaps some could employ canon. And some more challenging pieces may include partner tunes—or even two-part writing. But the difficulty of the anthem must not be such so that it obscures the teaching of healthy singing. So many common pitfalls of a children's choir can be avoided with thoughtful and quality repertoire! Feed children quality age-appropriate and musical repertoire, with text that is not silly (that's not to say it can't be fun) and, at the very least, text that makes theological and biblical sense.

If your church doesn't have a children's choir, could not the children of the church school form a youth choir? You could build into their weekly schedule an allotted time of singing that would include some basic teachings about worship and their role in it. You could sing through any choruses or responses or hymns that will occur in worship that week.

There are a plethora of resources to consult in your planning for involving children in worship and for helping those who lead a children's choir.[6] But the larger goals are to involve

---

[6]I recommend the excellent resource *A Child Shall Lead: A Sourcebook for Christian Educators, Musicians, and Clergy,* edited by John D. Witvliet (Garland, Tex.: Chorister's Guild, 1999). Available online at www.choristersguild.org.

children in worship in meaningful ways and to feed them quality literature, while at the same time teaching them about healthy singing.

"All God's children have a place in the choir," sings the old spiritual. We were all made to sing. Whether in a choir, praise team, chorus, children's choir, or ensemble, God's people love to sing together. When voices are added to voices, a wonderful result is achieved that blesses God and God's people—singers and hearers alike. But like all blessings, a responsibility is attached, namely, to use music to point to God, the One seated on the throne, who delights in our song.

QUESTIONS FOR REFLECTION AND DISCUSSION

1. Are you doing all you can, given your church's budget, tangible support, and personnel, to nourish and grow your choir or praise team? Are there some ways in which you can improve?

2. Complete this sentence: One thing I hope never changes about our choir or praise team is . . .

3. Complete this sentence: If I could remove one distraction from our choir or praise team, it would be . . .

4. Are there other ways (beyond what you've already tried) to involve your choir or praise team in worship? If so, what are they?

5. Are you involving children in worship? How might you involve them even more?

FIVE

Serving with an Instrument

All the Levites who were musicians—Asaph, Heman, Jeduthun and their sons and relatives—stood on the east side of the altar, dressed in fine linen and playing cymbals, harps and lyres. They were accompanied by 120 priests sounding trumpets. The trumpeters and singers joined in unison, as with one voice, to give praise and thanks to the LORD. Accompanied by trumpets, cymbals and other instruments, they raised their voices in praise to the LORD and sang:

> "He is good;
> his love endures forever."
>
> 2 CHRONICLES 5:12–13

LET EVERYTHING THAT HAS BREATH PRAISE THE LORD!

Being the gregarious folks that they are, Jon and Joy quickly met a new couple in church last Sunday. After inviting Nelson and Phyllis over for lunch and a swim in the pool, they discovered that the new couple possessed considerable musical gifts! Excited to pursue the conversation, Jon discovered that Nelson was an accomplished tuba player, and Phyllis admitted—when pushed—that she "kind of" knew how to read music.

Deflated, Jon and Joy dismissed the idea of inviting the guests to participate in their church's music program. For surely there wouldn't be a way to include them—or would there?

Most people, at one time or another, have played a musical instrument. As facilitators of worship, worship planners should look for opportunities to use people's instrumental skills in worship. Instrumentalists don't always have to be only professional musicians; all calibers of instrumental players can be involved effectively. For example, think back to Jon and Joy's guests. Nelson could be in a brass ensemble (a tuba is a wonderful addition, and even if a tuba part isn't offered in a score, tuba players can often use a trombone II score), and Phyllis, even though possessing minimal keyboard skills, could be a valuable member of a handbell choir.

It may be helpful to survey the congregation to discover the instrumentalists who belong to your church. In appendix 3 you'll find an instrumentalist survey that you may use as is or adapt for use in your service planning. You could advertise for instrumentalists in the church newsletter or by word of mouth or through a group e-mail message to church members. You might simply ask around. Once you've obtained the names and instruments of persons in your congregation, keep an accurate and up-to-date file you can tap in to when you come across music that calls for different instruments. Dedicate part of your music budget and file storage space to instrumental music, and organize the music according to woodwind, brass, strings, trumpet(s), and so forth.

(And don't forget to ask new members if they play an instrument. Your invitation may be just what they need to be more fully assimilated into the life and ministry of the church.)

BRASS INSTRUMENTS

Brass instrumentation is wonderful, adding a festive and regal air to the worship services. Especially with organ, the effect of brass instruments during congregational singing can be spine-tingling. I prefer to search for music for brass and organ that is used idiomatically—music that lets them use their idiom to the fullest through such means as fanfares, embellishments, and dotted rhythms.

Brass parts tend to work best when used in odd numbers. One trumpet on a part—or three (not two)—helps intonation and tone. Placement of a brass ensemble in the worship space is also critical. If at all possible, place the brass at right angles to the congregation. Second best is to have them play behind the congregation, supporting their singing. The last option is to place them in front, facing the congregation, since from that position their sound can easily overwhelm rather than enhance the singing.

STRINGED INSTRUMENTS

Strings offer unique and wonderful sounds. Violins support congregational singing well, and they can double soaring descant lines or countermelodies. Much solo literature is written for two violins (including Mozart's wonderful collections of church sonatas),[7] and for hymn singing, two violins can play soprano and another voice. Experiment with the strings playing around in octaves, too; for instance, have one violin play the melody of "Beautiful Savior," with the second violin playing the tenor line an octave higher. Three violins? You have the start of an orchestra! And remember that violins can either bow or use pizzicato (plucking) for different effects.

---

[7]Amadeus Wolfgang Mozart, *Church (Organ) Sonatas 1-8* (Bocan Raton, Fla.: Kalmus A 1109) and *Five Church Sonatas* (Bocan Raton, Fla.: Kalmus A 1110).

Bass violin players also offer bass support for hymn singing and anthems. They serve well with piano and in other ensembles. Try the pizzicato for different effects. Just remember that, like brass instruments, strings are most successful with an odd number of instruments on each part.

HANDBELLS

Handbells are most often used in churches in a choir setting (as a handbell choir). These groups offer much in worship by way of service music (prelude, offertory, or postlude) and provide many non-singers with a musical outlet to use their talents within the church's worship.

Although many directors limit the use of handbells just to the handbell anthem, they can be used along with other instruments or with organ for hymn accompaniments. Their bright ringing sound adds a wonderful texture to the singing. Free-ringing handbells provide another wonderful effect. Simply pull out the desired handbells (I like to use tones 1, 3, 5, and 6 in the key of the song) and give them to choir members or randomly selected folks from the congregation. On a chosen stanza, ask them to ring their bells randomly. "Chance" music at its finest! This works particularly well for big, festive hymns like "God of Grace and God of Glory," "Christ the Lord Is Risen Today," and "Joy to the World!"

The random bell ringing is even doable in churches that don't own a set of handbells. Try this: On Christmas Day and Easter Sunday, invite congregation members to bring their own bells from home. It doesn't matter if they're wooden, brass, crystal, or china. For the last stanza of the opening hymn, have

everyone who has brought a bell—wherever they are seated—
ring it! The variety of timbres spreading throughout the room
is a marvelous effect that will add new life to the opening hymn
for a festive day. And people will thank you for the invitation
to be involved. (Just be sure to ask people to place their bells
on the floor, well outside their reach, for the remainder of the
service.)

A lone handbell can be employed for more solemn worship
events. A tolling low-C can mark the hour to begin a Good Friday service; a repeated tolling G works well with the passion
hymn "Ah, Holy Jesus," and so forth.

WOODWIND INSTRUMENTS

Much repertoire is written for woodwind instruments and keyboard. Obviously, using these pieces for service music would be
a great place to start when bringing woodwinds into worship.
Since most woodwinds are C instruments, they can play directly
out of the songbook to accompany hymns and songs. But don't
forget to experiment a little: Could an oboe try the tenor line
up an octave? a flutist take the solo melody and lead the congregation as other instruments drop out? a saxophone add jazz
licks to "Jesus Loves Me"?

GUITARS

Guitars add harmonic and percussive texture when played with
a keyboard. Especially good for Spanish songs, guitars are
adaptable and versatile. Try adding a string bass player with guitar and piano (and a trumpet and percussion, if you have these

instrumentalists), and you'll have an instant mariachi band ready to bring Spanish songs to life.

Most modern hymnals and song sheets include guitar symbols in the score. But also try experimenting with your own varying harmonizations in order to give a new lift to the song.

HARPSICHORDS

One time a church I was serving received a harpsichord as a gift. The initial reaction wasn't overly positive: it was just another instrument to store—a fragile one and difficult to tune, to boot—and unlikely to be used.

We were, however, pleasantly surprised. The harpsichord is a keyboard instrument that makes it possible, and even fun, for all the church keyboardists to play. The pleasant, quiet tones of the harpsichord make it a wonderful accompanying instrument for both choirs and soloists—particularly when singing Baroque literature. When solo strings play in church, it is the perfect accompaniment instrument. For string quartets and small orchestras, it turns into a continuo instrument.

And I haven't even yet mentioned one of the harpsichord's best features: it's portable! You can place it in the worship space wherever it's needed. One word of caution: Like a piano or organ, you get what you pay for with a harpsichord. It may be best to consult an expert before purchasing a harpsichord.

PERCUSSION INSTRUMENTS

Probably no instrument receives more complaints than drums—probably because drums, congas, and drum sets are often not judiciously used, as well as because some people make negative associations with drums. Percussion serves best as a texture to accompanying instruments, and sensitive percussionists add, not detract, from the ensemble. When using drums, less is more. Many drummers subconsciously use repetitive patterns for all songs, regardless of the genre. Percussionists wanting to expand their menu of patterns may want to study the difference, say, between a bossa nova and calypso rhythm. Rather than keeping beat on a certain song, perhaps percussionists would want to use percussive effects—brushes, wind chimes, gong, and so forth. Again, the idea is to *add* to the worship of God, not cause any kind of distraction. Timpani (sometimes called kettledrums) would be my first percussion purchase of choice. Just three timpani drums (tuned to the tonic, subdominant, and dominant tones of the key) add a regal touch to any brass ensemble repertoire. And don't forget the hymns! With these three timpani drums, most hymns and songs could gain great benefit. Solo timpani rolling and crescendoing a low tonic note for a few measures would be a dramatic effect before the other instrumentalists joined for the hymn introduction. Then saving the timpani for the final chorus would be a stunning climatic touch.

MORE IDEAS!

Have an autoharp? Try using one for early American hymns; the sound is just right, and it's easy to pull off for almost anyone who can read music or follow chord symbols. For more Early American flavor, add a violin (fiddle) or flute to carry or embellish the melody. If you're concerned that the autoharp won't project well in the sanctuary, place it over a metal garbage can (really!), and you'll have an instant resonator.

Cymbals borrowed from the local high school marching band can add a wonderful celebrative "clap" to the end of a big hymn. If brass and organ are playing, all the better. Be careful, though, not to overuse the effect; believe me, a little cymbal crash goes a long way!

Hand percussion instruments are affordable and easy to use. I like to have a percussion box always on hand, filled with tambourines, woodblocks, sand blocks, triangles, shakers, and the like. When practicing Sunday's songs with the choir or praise team, try a few different percussion effects (if it fits the musical style) to add new life to the song. Let players improvise their own rhythm patterns. Add and subtract instruments to your liking.

Orff instruments also increase the musical palette. Named after the famed musician Carl Orff, who wanted to find a way to have all children participate successfully in making music, Orff instruments are xylophones, metallophones, and glockenspiels. The beauty of these instruments is not only their sound but also the fact that unused keys can be removed, thereby lessening the chance of player mistakes. Children love to play with these instruments, and we can let them play along on certain hymns in worship! If you have an ensemble of instruments, an arrangement of various ostinato patterns could be worked out to support congregational singing. If, however, only one or two instruments are available, then it'd be best to have a keyboard instrument lead the congregation, with Orff instruments providing another texture.

Wind chimes are one of my favorite effects for Christmas Eve. Either borrowed from someone's garden or purchased at a music store, wind chimes add a haunting but warm effect to carols such as "Silent Night, Holy Night" and "O Little Town of Bethlehem." Have someone in the congregation strike or strum the wind chimes just a few times during the introduction to and singing of these carols.

Using recorders (most often soprano, but also available in alto, tenor, and bass) is another easy way to involve more people—including children—in a new ensemble. Recorders are easy to hold and play. With a flute sound, they can double melody lines of songs or play descants. As an ensemble they can play alone, using parts and different size recorders, or in an instrumental ensemble they can add a medieval quality to early hymnody.

In surveying all the modern instruments available for use, I've been careful to point out ways in which instruments can assist in the hymn accompaniments. This is crucial. To use instruments exclusively for prelude, offertory, and postlude music serves only to reinforce a performance model of participation and may actually discourage other players who don't want to "play solo." The use of instruments to add texture and variety to songs heightens the praise of God by illuminating text in a new way.

QUESTIONS FOR REFLECTION AND DISCUSSION

1. How can you better assess your talent pool of instrumentalists within the congregation?

2. Do you include everyone who has an interest in participating, or do you tend to use the same musicians and instruments?

3. Could you involve children with such instruments as bells or percussion or Orff instruments? If so, how and when could this begin, and who could help bring it about?

SIX

Serving in the Pew

The dearest idol I have known,
Whate'er that idol be,
Help me to tear it from Thy throne
And worship only Thee.

WILLIAM COWPER

HOW TO WORSHIP WELL
WITH HEART AND MIND

Our imaginary friends Jon and Joy have let us enter their lives by means of this book. While by and large they represent church musicians and church members, in some ways they are distinct—they have found their place in the church, and this place gives them purpose and meaning. Their involvement in the music program enriches their worship and their lives.

To a culture wallowing in banality, superficiality, and violence, worship holds out the promise of a divine encounter, an encounter with the One who is known and the One who yet remains mysterious, requiring us to live by faith and not by sight. With scientific advances that boggle the mind and with technological possibilities growing at exponential rates, there's little room in our shrinking world, it seems, for the unknown. We have life figured out.

Yet we have seen how music leads the congregation in worship and in song. We use music to express the awe-inspiring as well as the unutterable. We use music to gather the congregation and to send them forth with a bounce in their step. We use music to accompany our texts of praise and to introduce these songs. We are stewards of music on behalf of all the members of the congregation.

What an amazing thing it is to sing our songs of praise to God together. Think about this: In a fractured world that seems to be spinning out of control in every direction, and even within the church, which is all too often fractured by controversy, singing is the one thing the congregation can do that is beautiful and unified. It is a team activity that draws everyone together while giving harmonious praise to God. Haven't you experienced those wonderful times of singing, when the sound of many voices washed over you like a wave, rising and dipping, lifting and carrying your own small voice up into that larger harmony? In the church, no one sings alone.

Sadly, not all people are blessed to have the experience of meaningful involvement. It's rare to find a group activity that is not entertainment- or sports-related in our culture.

HOW TO SING WELL

Given such an important and symbolic activity, we ought to learn to sing well. For congregations who want to sing well and for musicians who want to lead their congregations to sing well, we can do no better than to look at John Wesley's instructions given to his congregation in 1761:[8]

I. Learn these tunes before you learn any others; afterwards learn as many as you please.

II. Sing them exactly as they are printed here, without altering or mending them at all; and if you have

---

[8]From the preface of John Wesley's *Sacred Melody*, 1761.

learned to sing them otherwise, unlearn them as soon as you can.

III. Sing all. See that you join with the congregation as frequently as you can. Let not a slight degree of weakness or weariness hinder you. If it is a cross to you, take it up, and you will find it a blessing.

IV. Sing lustily and with a good courage. Beware of singing as if you were half dead, or half asleep, but lift up your voice with strength. Be no more afraid of your voice now, nor more ashamed of its being heard, than when you sang the songs of Satan.

V. Sing modestly. Do not bawl, so as to be heard above or distinct from the rest of the congregation, that you may not destroy the harmony, but strive to unite your voices together, so as to make one clear, melodious sound.

VI. Sing in time. Whatever time is sung, be sure to keep with it. Do not run before nor stay behind it, but attend close to the leading voices, and move therewith as exactly as you can; and take care not to sing too slow. This drawling way naturally steals on all who are lazy, and it is high time to drive it out from among us, and sing all our tunes just as quick as we did at first.

VII. Above all, sing spiritually. Have an eye to God in every word you sing. Aim at pleasing Him more than yourself, or any other creature. In order to do this, attend strictly to the sense of what you sing, and see that your heart is not carried away with the sound but offered to God continually; so shall your singing be such as the Lord will approve of here, and reward you when He cometh in the clouds of heaven.

Congregations who desire to sing well educate themselves. Through adult education classes, sermon series on worship and praise, hymn festivals, church newsletter articles, journals, and magazines, congregations learn to grow in appreciation for the songs they offer in worship. We often erroneously conclude that our hymns are part of the biblical canon; they're not. All hymns and songs—with the exception of canticles (biblical songs set to music) and psalms—are poetry and music written by fellow Christians. We ought to educate ourselves about the occasion, the use, and the intention of the songs we offer in worship so that we can use them appropriately and with a right understanding. As in all things, education increases appreciation.

For example, I once knew an organist who programmed Bach's chorale prelude on "Christ Jesus Lay in Death's Strong Bands" for each Good Friday service. His understanding was that it was a piece for Good Friday; looking only at the title, he assumed that the piece was about Jesus, bound in grave clothes and lying in a tomb. What he didn't know (or had failed to research) was the next line of the hymn: "But now at God's right hand He stands and brings us life from heaven."[9] This is an Easter text! To further muddle things, his Lenten interpretation of Bach's piece was executed with a dirge tempo and with the quietest stops of the organ. Done appropriately, the piece should have been triumphant, if not whimsical.

Also, just because a piece of music exists doesn't mean it has an inherent right to be used in worship. Church musicians and worship planners also evaluate and discern what will work best for their particular community of faith. They use the best

---

[9]Words by Martin Luther (1483-1546).

resources to bring the music to life and select quality repertoire that is worthy of worship.

The point is that we need to educate ourselves about the hymnody we use. One way to educate the congregation is to find and use teachable moments. A great idea is to plan a hymn festival—a special worship service that uses hymns and songs to illumine a certain theme. My favorite idea came from an innovative man named Hal Hopson, who built a hymn festival that had each hymn writer "appear" in costume to explain his or her hymn.[10] Imagine Johann Sebastian Bach appearing behind your lectern to tell the congregation about the writing of his chorales. Or imagine Miriam, Moses' sister, dancing up and down the aisles with her tambourine as she explains the occasion for her song in Exodus after Pharaoh's horses and riders were thrown into the sea. This hymn festival idea can increase our understanding of the music of songs, while giving a greater appreciation of the text and what occasioned its writing. It is worship and it provides a teachable moment—all at once. Kids especially love it. They can enter into the experience and are intrigued by the costumed hymn writers.

For hymn festivals, the ideas are endless, as are the different kinds of themes you could select for hymn festivals. The point is that God's people primarily offer during worship their praise through song. Congregations who ignore musical education, creativity, and excellence do so at their own peril.

---

[10]Hal Hopson in *Chorister Guild Letters* (Winter 1998); see also Randall D. Engle, "Songwriters Tell Their Stories," in *Reformed Worship* 54 (December 1999), 36–40.

Here are a number of questions to ask of ourselves as musicians and as congregational members to increase the intentionality and quality of our praise:

1. *Do we worship with reverence and with awe?* When we come into God's presence in a special way during the worship service, when we pray and sing and participate in the sacraments (or ordinances), do we sense that we are dealing with the things of God? Do we treat this time as an hour set apart, or are we simply getting through the hour, just as we would any other hour of the week?

2. *How do we prepare for worship?* It's amazing to read in the Old Testament of the elaborate and complex preparations for worship. No one in those days just jumped in the car and scurried off to church! But I wonder if the preparation, time, and thought invested by the saints of old to prepare for worship were such bad things. Personally speaking, what continually amazes me is the connection between my *attitude* (my mental preparation) going into worship and my *experience* in that time of worship. How do we prepare our hearts for worship?

Some churches use written prompts to remind worshipers about what they've come to do. Bulletin or overhead reminders (such as, "We use this gathering music to prepare our hearts and minds for worship") may help in this regard. No matter how we do it, we need to see worship as an engagement with God and prepare ourselves for it appropriately.

3. *Does worship make us better people?* This question may appear radically out of place in this book; after all, worship is not about us, it's about God. Yet we also recognize that to meet God is to be changed by God, to be transformed as a result of knowing and loving him. Worship reorients us. We see things

anew, from a new vantage point. God reminds us who is at the center, and we leave our times of worship readjusted to that reality.

4. *Do we sing our songs of praise "with all our heart and with all our mind"?* Praise, as we have seen, is at the heart of Christian worship. We ought to learn to do it well. Have we enthusiastically entered into the song of God's people? Do we give our time and talents to the worship program through our special gifts? If our gifts are not musical, have we at least encouraged those who lead us in music and in worship and given them the resources to do their work well?

5. *Are we teaching our children how to worship?* As the old adage says, "More often than not, learning is caught, not taught." We teach our children with our words but also with our actions. Do they see us participating in worship? Do we talk to them about worship, explaining its meaning and rhythm? Do they regularly attend worship? Can our church add a component of worship education to its church school curriculum? The church cannot rely on any other institution to teach our children about worship—or about the faith, for that matter. It is up to us. It is our joy and our responsibility to teach them the joy of worship. How are we doing?

6. *Is our worship worship?* Worship is about awe, not about strategy. Many churches want worship to *do* something for them: to educate (at the center of worship is not God's throne but a lectern), to soothe (the throne is replaced by a psychiatrist's couch), to evangelize (a revival tent replaces the throne), or to entertain (the throne is replaced by a recital hall). It's not that worship can't teach or soothe, evangelize or delight—but aren't these by-products of worship? To declare Jesus Christ's

worth-ship is the heart of worship and the reason for its exis-
tence. Is our worship truly worship?

7. *Are we supporting our music and worship program with ade-
quate funding?* Given such a central and important function, the
significance of worship ought to be reflected in the church's
ministry plan and in the church budget. Does our budget provide enough resources for us to do worship well?

Some may object to spending money "just on music"—on
what appears to them to be nonessential things. "After all," the
logic goes, "think of all the good this money could do else-
where in ministry." Of course, it may very well be true. A church
ministry plan should balance worship with other kingdom-
building activity. Yet many churches quickly and lavishly fund
ministries such as youth programs and fellowship activities
while making short shrift of the worship budget. Recall the
wonderful story of Jesus and the woman with the jar of per-
fume worth about a year's wages. She splashed her gift on Jesus'
feet. Then it was gone. It was extravagant. It was wasteful. And
all it was good for was the praise and worship of Jesus. The dis-
ciples chided her with the same logic—"think of all the poor
people we could have fed!" Jesus commended her, "She has
done a beautiful thing to me." Jesus reminds us that worship is
important, and it is beautiful. It is necessary.

To do worship well will take financial resources. Is the
importance of worship reflected in our budget?

8. *Do we leave worship having seen the picture of the circle of
praise around God's throne?* We end where we began—with God's
throne. Worship brings us into an encounter with God, who is
beyond our capacity to fully grasp and understand. Worship
brings us face-to-face with Jesus, the author and perfecter of our

faith. And there, somehow, in his awesome majesty and power, God does not overwhelm us or make us feel guilty all over again. God holds us. God receives us. And God delights in our thanksgiving and in our praise.

We worship.

> Then I heard every creature in heaven and on earth and under the earth and on the sea, and all that is in them, singing:
>
> "To him who sits on the throne and to the Lamb
> be praise and honor and glory and power,
>> forever and ever!"
>
> The four living creatures said, "Amen," and the elders fell down and worshiped.   Revelation 5:13–14

QUESTIONS FOR REFLECTION AND DISCUSSION

1. How can you better educate your congregation about worship?

2. What are your short-term and long-term goals to enhance the praise of your congregation? Think about such things as education for adults and youth, hymn festivals, quality and variety of instrumentation, the acoustics of the worship space (is it conducive for singing?), and different musical groups and ensembles that could be formed or that need enhancing.

3. What do you make of the author's proposition that singing is the central mode of human praise? Are there other ways you could praise God beyond the singing human voice—drama, liturgical dance, readers' groups, and so forth? How could you use these talents to point to God's throne?

APPENDIX 1

A Church Musician's Prayer

Church music is for you, God.

I praise you, God, for every gift in our possession, because each gift presumes a giver and each ability finds its origin in God's creativity. Without God's joy, there would be no song worth singing. Without the gift of music, we would not know the art of making music or the extreme delight in using word and sound to God's glory.

God is our theme. We can never exhaust so vast a subject. By God's Spirit we find new meaning in old songs, and new songs are born out of the constant freshness of God's Word.

I thank you, God,

- ❏ for the rich heritage of music from the past.
- ❏ for poets whose words sing twice over when they are set to music.
- ❏ for the composers of today, who are adding to the rich legacy we already possess.
- ❏ for variety, innovation, and the mix of taste and talent that keeps our church from stagnation and familiarity.
- ❏ for those whose gift it is to use their voice or instrument to create the atmosphere of worship.
- ❏ for those who taught us our expertise, who urged us to study, and who continue to urge us to improve our skills.
- ❏ for the joy of leading the congregation's song.
- ❏ for the joy of assisting the choir to find their special voice.

I shun

- ❏ making music into a god to be worshiped for its own sake.
- ❏ carelessly performing music unfit for God's praise.
- ❏ drawing attention to myself rather than pointing to God.
- ❏ musical snobbery.
- ❏ sentimentality.
- ❏ neglect of the meaning of a song.
- ❏ singing without personal commitment to God.

I pray that church musicians will be servants, cooperating with other musicians and the congregation to lead in both the solemnity and exuberance of true worship.

Worship Planning Checklist

Photocopy several copies and use weekly at worship planning sessions

The Givens:

Date: _____

Sunday of church year: _____

Worship leader(s): _____

Preacher: _____

Musicians: _____

Ushers: _____

Greeters: _____

The Theme:

Preacher's Scripture text: _____

Complementary texts: _____

Church year theme (Advent, Lent, and so forth): _____

_____

Sacraments (ordinances) celebrated today: _____

_____

Has the choir or soloist already selected their song(s)? If so,
they are: _____

_____

Our Songs:

Write down all song ideas that would be appropriate (psalm
settings, hymns, choruses, songs, spirituals, children's songs,
canticles): _____

_____

_____

_____

_____

How many songs will be used this week? _____

Narrow down the choices (remember, "something old, something borrowed, and something blue"): _____

_____

_____

_____

_____

_____

_____

The Plan:

Instrumentalists needed: _____

Vocalists needed: _____

Descants available: _____

Soloist/choir/praise team needed to introduce new songs:

_____

Choir anthem(s): _____

Other harmonizations available or needed: _____

_____

Service music: prelude, offertory, postlude. Other? _____

_____

For Further Thought:

❏ Are there ways to sing the songs creatively? Soloist only on particular stanzas, men only on a stanza, canon style, no accompaniment, and so forth?

❏ Is there a way to visually enhance our worship space so as to complement this theme?

❏ Could our artisans aid in worship this week?

  ✔ Compose a new song?

  ✔ Create cover art for the bulletin?

  ✔ Enhance the space with color, sculpture, or a symbolic montage?

❏ Communication:

  ✔ Have we put the order together in a logical flow?

  ✔ Is the order of worship clearly laid out and printed?

  ✔ How will we communicate today's decisions to all involved?

  ✔ Who will be responsible to touch base with the organist, pianist, instrumentalists, choir director, pastor, secretary, and custodian?

APPENDIX 3

Instrumentalists' Survey

Our church is excited about utilizing everyone's talents in worship. We are currently in the process of identifying all our instrumentalists. Would you take a moment to complete this survey?

Name: _____

Phone: _____

E-mail Address: _____ @ _____

In worship, I would be willing to play:

❏ Autoharp
❏ Cello
❏ Clarinet
❏ Flute
❏ French Horn
❏ Guitar
❏ Harp
❏ Keyboard
❏ Oboe
❏ Organ
❏ Percussion
❏ Piano
❏ String Bass
❏ Trombone

❏ Trumpet

❏ Tuba

❏ Viola

❏ Violin

❏ Xylophone

❏ Other (specify): _____

I'd rate my ability as (circle one)

excellent   good   so-so   I haven't played in years!

I own, but don't play anymore, the following instruments:

_____

_____

_____

Would you consider allowing the church to borrow this instrument sometime? _____

Printed in the United States
7934/LV000009B/5

concentration of the full lips, the light sheen of sweat on her working muscles. He found himself gravitating toward the mental image of a smaller, more delicate form in the same position, that small mouth less than a foot from his aching balls. Amazingly, that image tightened his loins in a way that standing right over Tamara's lithe form and hearing her open invitation did not.

Regardless, he suspected Violet would be hard-pressed to believe he was thinking of her if he got a hard-on right now. In fact, he figured she'd probably pistol whip him until his head caved in before he managed an explanation. He grinned at the thought and changed the direction of his thoughts, just to be safe.

"So where is your sister today?"

"Oh, she just went off shift. She was supposed to meet Marguerite for lunch at the Tea Room. Marguerite runs the place, and we're thinking of integrating a classy coffee room here at the club. You know, for clients to enjoy after they have their workout, socialize some more. A kind of franchise of the Tea Room inside of our club. She left a few minutes ago."

"You both work here?"

"She does. I'm actually the owner, she's the manager, so I can pretty much just show up, work out and handle the stockholders. She handles day-to-day stuff in the club. She likes to do that versus any of the aggressive sales stuff, and I hate being bogged down in maintenance and repair details and breaking people into the machines. That's why she's going to see Marguerite. She's working out the details with her now that I've closed the deal."

"You're a good complement to each other, then."

"The joy of being twins." She nodded, and he helped her take it back up to the rack. She sat up, considered him, gave him another sultry smile and a perusal so blatant it had some of the surrounding customers raising a brow or grinning.

"If you ever change your mind, hon, my sister and I'd love to sink our teeth into you. I suspect you're the meal of a lifetime."

"Again, I'm flattered." He inclined his head. "But I think it's fair to say…I'm off the market as long as my — "

He stumbled to a halt. He'd forgotten, and he never forgot. But he'd almost said it aloud, called Violet what his mind had accepted her as. His Mistress. Of heart, mind and soul. Just as she'd said from the very first she would become to him.

"…I'm otherwise involved."

Tamara rose, running her hand familiarly up his thigh, over his hip bone and to his waist. "Our loss, hon. Maybe Violet will share you with us again sometime." Then she left him, drawing the attention of every patron with her African queen looks and the lithe body displayed in the shimmering spandex.

"I hope not," he muttered.

It was getting easier to admit that now. He wanted to be committed to one Mistress, and her to him. While some interactive play was fine, he wanted the main event, the focus, just to be with her. As long as he had Violet, he wouldn't care if he never saw the inside of a BDSM club again.

However, he had other issues to deal with at the moment. Kiera and Tamara worked as a team. Nothing about the crime scene suggested more than one player in

the room with the vic at the time of death. He had written off Lisbeth right away. The woman was as frank and honest about herself as she was with her subs. She didn't have any demons in her closet and seemed to have little interest in a man young enough to be her son. There were the five female Doms with permanent memberships, but he was particularly interested in Marguerite Perruquet.

He'd watched her pick up a twenty-something at The Zone the last night he was there. She'd kept the young man at her foot like a pet dog, lapping sparkling tonic water out of a bowl while she talked to other Doms, occasionally slapping him on the ass with a sharp quirt she carried, tucked into a metal band on her forearm. But when she took him down to play in one of the rooms, that cruelty turned to dangerous gentility. She'd put him on a turnstile, raised it vertical, spun him upside down so he could eat her clit, then strapped a cock to his head and made him coordinate fucking her with it while he licked at the base of her pussy, nibbled her thighs. All the while she teased his cock, positioned at her eye level, with her mouth, her teeth, working him and threatening him, telling him he could not come until she did. By the end of two hours, she had made him come for her several times, in a variety of ways where she was alternately playful and vicious, loving and cruel, until Mac understood why she was a Mistress of great popularity at The Zone. A sub's only regret with her would be that she rarely chose the same man for more than one night.

Or maybe she did, but her pickups for longer term relationships didn't occur at The Zone, and those she hooked up with weren't ever going to be able to talk about it.

The early evening crowd thinned, and he went to the locker room before his lingering became suspicious. Police investigative work was ninety percent tedium, two percent clues and eight percent hunches. Of course, this case had been a little less tedious because of Violet. He'd cook her up a quiche tonight. He'd seen what was in her fridge and knew she lived on frozen food. Not anymore.

Once in street clothes and headed for his bike, he was annoyed to see he was parked diagonally from Powell's Lexus, and the arrogant dickhead was in the process of putting a gym bag in his trunk.

Mac passed him with a cold nod and the blond shot him a baleful look as Mac picked up his helmet to straddle the Honda.

"You know what I don't get about you, Mac? You play the game all wrong."

"Not interested, Powell," he said briefly, fitting his key into the ignition.

"You don't get it, Mac. And I thought you would. It's obvious you don't like to give up power, but you resist it out front. I play the game in reverse. They think I'm all theirs, I give them everything they want until the end, indulge every whim, and then when they lose their hearts, I cut them loose. It's a power rush like you wouldn't believe. These Mistresses, they salivate all over you. You could choose any of them, but you get yourself tied up emotionally over a little inexperienced cunt like Violet. All you're really looking for is a ring in your nose. You're not fooling anyone."

"Powell, I'm not going to brawl with you like two kids in a school yard. Skip the goading insults and tell me what you want."

Powell stepped forward and, sensing trouble coming, Mac got off the bike to face him.

"You got me kicked out of The Zone. You're welcome to your opinion but not the right to interfere in my personal dealings."

"Wrong. Protecting a woman, even if she's not his own, is every man's business."

Jonathan sneered. "If she'd chosen me, she'd be so twisted around my dick by now she might as well be on her knees sucking on it."

"You're an asshole, and what burns you is that Violet didn't choose you. She's beautiful, she has taste, and she knows trouble when she sees it. You don't need a Mistress. You need to be neutered."

He knew how to handle an idiot like Powell, so he was ready for the lunge, the swipe of Powell's fist, his keys clutched in them. But Mac was angry as well. Not enough to let it control him, but enough for him to take a split second to consider and then take great satisfaction in following up his block with a clip to Jonathan's jaw. Powell sagged forward and Mac caught him. The sharp jab in his neck spun him around, and he was vaguely aware of Jonathan regaining his balance at his back as Kiera pulled the syringe out.

There was no time for anything. The helmet dropped from his fingers and his body fell into their hands. They effectively used his momentum to roll him into the open door of the van next to his bike. All over in five seconds, and likely not a person around to see it. Jesus Christ, he was in trouble.

* * * * *

"Wake up, sweet thing. Wake up."

The soft crooning of the gentle voice was as melodious as a Motown lullaby, but it brought Mac back to consciousness like a cold spike shoved into his vitals. It took his mind a moment to catch up with the reaction, but the abrupt attempt to lunge to his feet got him nowhere.

He was in Tyler's dungeon, secured over the large spanking bench, stripped naked. Bolted securely to the floor, the bench didn't even quiver when he yanked against his bonds. His waist was on the edge of the bench, his knees pressed into the cold floor. An iron bar attached to a strap around his legs just above each knee held his thighs apart, wide enough that the position caused painful tension in his lower back, buttocks and thighs. He was hyperaware that the position made his cock and balls hang out free and accessible to anything anyone wanted to do to them.

Close to the juncture between testicle and leg, another strap had been buckled around each thigh. His wrists were cuffed and the rings on those cuffs clipped to the straps, so his arms were held immobile at his sides. He had no way to protect his skull from the single bullet he was sure the woman somewhere beyond his field of vision intended to put into it. His head was unsupported over the edge of the bench, his neck muscles groaning in protest.

"Would you like to hear my secrets, Mac? The ones you've been trying so hard to figure out?"

Her voice stayed whisper soft. He knew that type of voice, knew the ice that climbed up his spine from hearing it was not an overreaction.

"I'd rather have you turn me loose," he said mildly, "but since I suspect that's out of the question, go for it."

Blab all you want. Give me some time to think, figure out what chance I've got not to be vic number four.

"You try to play it down," she observed, "But I know how miserable you are. How miserable all of us are. But a Dom cannot escape the pain. She must face it, help her slaves find a release to it, ironically through the experience of physical pain. Do you know what the source of all of it is?"

Mac shook his head. "No."

Abruptly his back was on fire, as a lash came down on it from somewhere behind him. Hooked with barbed tips, it took his flesh with it when it was yanked away.

"No, *Mistress*," she snapped.

Swearing through a haze of pain, Mac bared his teeth. "You're not my Mistress, bitch, so beat me to death, you won't hear it from my lips."

He heard the movement of air as an arm was drawn back for another strike, but the blow did not come. Ten tense seconds passed before she spoke again, and this time her voice was laced with amusement.

"As we told Violet, you're a treasure. Jonathan, please put down the cat and go get the other item I wanted to use."

As Jonathan's footsteps retreated, Kiera's came closer, and then she was in his field of vision, standing before him. She wore a black unitard, no jewelry, her hair slicked back from her face, her boots laced securely to her thighs. Latex black gloves covered her hands up to her elbows. She took a seat on the couch, crossed her legs and laid an arm along the back, as if she had nothing but time, but her eyes had a singular intensity that felt like she was drilling holes in his head already.

"So where is your sister? Is she part of this unholy trinity?"

"Mac," she said, "you don't need to worry about being a cop. You're going to be dead shortly, and all that matters is you'll be free of pain, of having to hide who you are."

"I admit, Jonathan surprises me. *You're* not a tremendous surprise, all in all, but he is."

"Oh, there are even more startling things than that." Powell's footsteps returned. Mac jerked away at the rough touch on his jaw, but it was a futile gesture. Jonathan merely wrenched back his head with enough force to sprain muscles and shoved the ball gag into Mac's mouth, strapping it tightly around his head.

Kiera watched them impassively, then waved Jonathan back. "Give him ten lashes, love, to focus him on what I'm about to tell him, and then I want you to go cuff your left hand and left foot on the St. Andrew's cross. I'll come finish binding you in a moment. We want to be all ready to play when Mistress Violet gets here."

That cold hand around his intestines tightened exponentially and Mac's lips lifted in a snarl he could not voice around the gag.

"Ten, Mistress? With the barb?"

"Yes. Don't worry, love. I told you, he likes pain. Violet will be fine with it."

She looked down at Mac, the corner of her mouth curving. Those large dark eyes were trapped somewhere between lust and pain. Both characteristics obviously dwelled within her in such phenomenal quantities that it was like looking at a person with a demon inside her. The monster was far larger than the body housing it, so that it

made every word she said seem distorted, every facial expression an obscene aberration. It was something Mac was sure Powell could not see. He could, because in his line of work, he had seen it up close and personal. A person so far gone in death, blood and their own pain that there was nothing that could save them.

"I told Jonathan how you and I used to play together, and that you enjoyed kidnap scenarios," she said evenly. "I asked Tyler to leave Violet a message this morning, before he went out of town on his book tour, asking her to meet me here this evening for a very special surprise for her. Tyler's very generous with his dungeon for those he trusts, and Tamara and I have used it often. Jonathan rather hates you, so he wasn't keen on helping fulfill one of your fantasies at first. Then I told him you didn't really have any set boundaries, though I'd discovered there are certain things you truly dislike. So my gift to Jonathan for helping was going to be letting him fuck you in the ass. Jonathan's not really into men, but he does have an appreciation for the things that can cut someone's ego down to size, and I personally will enjoy seeing you suffer a bit. He really is like a Dom in sub clothing, a sort of twisted one, but an interesting specimen altogether." A fond look came into her eyes at something Mac was glad he could not see. "Look at him. He's getting hard, just thinking about it. Jonathan, do my bidding."

"With pleasure, Mistress."

Mac sunk his teeth into the heavy rubber of the gag as the metal barb tips struck his back, jerked off more flesh.

Kiera watched him, her face detached. She was in a place where she was seeing things that weren't visible to the rest of them, Mac knew, and it did not seem to bring

her any joy, just a grim purpose that boded ill for all of them.

"I can lash you so you'll feel the pain, but it won't draw blood. Jonathan has less experience at that. You'll just have to live with the scarring, at least for a short time." She blinked once.

A second and third strike fell, and Mac felt the pain jolt through his body like electrical current. His shoulder began to itch, as blood made its way down his back over his biceps, getting slowed in the hair on his arms.

"Very few can take it without screaming, but I know you can. Violet is going to be so impressed with your stamina."

The last stroke fell a few moments later, when all of them had merged into one vibrating field of pain on his back. Just as he released his breath, an eleventh came, striking across his ass, a barb catching his scrotum. His incisors sank down, slicing through the hard rubber, the reaction singing up through his gums and jaw.

"Jonathan, that was very naughty. Go cuff yourself."

"Yes, Mistress. My apologies, Mistress." Jonathan snickered.

The pain was unbelievable, worse than being shot, and for this there was no adrenaline kick in, nothing but throbbing, tearing agony.

"Now that you're paying attention, I'm going to tell you my secrets," she said, rising. She squatted down next to Mac and stroked her hand over his hair with her long fingers, following his cheekbone with her nail, pressing down a little hard, watching him as she traced the soft skin just below the vulnerable right eye. Mac kept his gaze steady on hers.

There was no fear now, only fury. He wouldn't give her fear, which meant he couldn't think about Violet getting here. He had to resolve this before then, one way or another.

"You know I like to mix potions. That cat was tipped in a very special mixture I make to punish my baddest boys. It's an alcohol base, mixed with a derivative of crushed nettle juice. Highly irritating, isn't it? It will keep hurting this badly all the way up to the last moment."

She brought her head down closer, so she could speak softly, where Jonathan could not hear. "I don't like to make my subs suffer just for the sake of pain. I draw their pain from them and then I release them with that one shot to the head. You're going to know it's coming, but I didn't want it that way. I don't want to hurt you except in ways that will give you release, focus you on what's important." She glanced toward Jonathan, now cuffed and waiting for her to finish restraining him, making him as helpless as Mac. "But him I intend to shoot between the eyes. Give him a full minute to see it coming, because he's a heartless bastard. Justice can be almost as invigorating as mercy killings, hmm?"

She smiled, feathering his hair off his forehead, as if she were stroking a puppy. "Lord, you are magnificent, you know that? I don't know what it is about you. I suppose you're thinking, Tyler will know who did this. Yes. Yes, he will. So I suppose I'll have to wait for him to come home and take care of that, just as I'll take care of Violet. I'm thinking I'll make it look like one of those 'sad, perverted life' stories. Erotica writer, living on the fringe of society, of reality, plays sick sex games with friends, offs them before he offs himself. And oh..." She put her fingers to her lips, her eyes widening. "One of them is Tampa's

finest, a homicide detective who was working undercover to find the S&M killer, and got too close because, he too, sadly, was part of that sick S&M scene. I'm sure that will result in a full departmental investigation, because how could we allow our fine police force to be infiltrated by such a sexual deviant?"

She stroked her finger down the line of his throat, her voice softening. "For you see, that's the problem. We all know what we are, but the world will never accept us. Would you like to hear a sad story?"

I'd like to put you out of your misery before Violet gets here, he thought grimly. How long did he have? Ten minutes? Five? An hour? If Violet had gone downstate to visit her mother, she might not get back until late afternoon, early evening, and then it was ninety minutes to Tyler's from Tampa. He tried not to think what Kiera could do to him in that amount of time, since she'd managed to inflict some serious damage in less than thirty seconds, but it would give him more time to plot a way to stop her before Violet got here. Or maybe Violet wouldn't come. Maybe she'd left a message on his machine that she'd decided to stay overnight at her mom's, or was running late.

Christ, Nighthorse. Focus. Powell's out of the picture, so figure out a way to overpower her. While hogtied to a bench bolted to the floor. Good trick.

"Tamara tried to tell me from the beginning. You see, she knew when we were twelve what she was. I was her first submissive. I delighted in pleasing her, whether it was eating her pussy under the sheets at night, or doing her homework, or giving her my share of Halloween candy. I could sit at her feet for hours just for the pleasure of her touch on my hair. But she trained me to be a

Mistress with her, to understand what it was to release people's emotions through pain, enjoy the sensuality of that, the give and take. When to hold the reins tight, when to let a sub have his head and when to put it to good use." Her lips curved. "One of them came to be quite dear to me. Long after Tamara was bored with him. She didn't really approve of us playing separately, so I had to hide my times with him. It made it even more exciting." Her eyes grew darker and Mac watched the changes in inflection, learning everything he could about her changes in mood and what they meant.

"But I wanted more. For the first time in my life. I wanted to wake up with a man around me in the morning. Silly, wasn't it? Totally impossible for people like us. T told me, over and over, but sometimes the heart just doesn't listen, does it?

"I told him what I wanted, and he said he couldn't. That he loved me, but eventually he was going to have to give up the scene and settle down with someone vanilla, that there was no way he could live his life like this forever and get where he wanted in his career. I lost my pride. I told him I could do that, would do that for him. He cried, told me that 'together we'd always want to play the game.' I could see how much it hurt him, what we could never have but wanted so much. It tore me to pieces.

"It was inevitable that she found out about him, of course. I'm a Mistress, but I'm her sub, and your Mistress always knows everything you're thinking. You and Violet aren't there yet, but you would have been, you already sensed it coming. I broke down and told Tamara everything, the pain was so awful, his rejection.

"She loves me, has always looked after me, so she pretended she was me, went to his parents, told them

what he was. Of course, it was his worst nightmare. Or so he always said it would be."

Her expression shifted, became dreamy, the closest to tranquility Mac had yet seen reflected in her face. "Tamara called me, told me to come over to his apartment, that she needed to show me something." She turned those soft brown eyes to him again. "You remember *Bambi*, the original book by Felix Salten, not the Disney whitewashed version? When the stag comes to get Bambi, to show him Man, with a capital 'M', lying dead on the forest floor, shot in a hunting accident? And Bambi is so afraid to get close, because the idea of Man was larger than life to him, something beyond his understanding. I was afraid like that when I walked into the room, smelled the blood. I was so afraid, because he was an extension of who I am, and if it had become too much for him, it would become too much for me. I was doomed. But Tamara made me come look at him, look at his face.

"He had shot himself, and was lying on the bed, curled up as if sleeping. There were thin tracks dried on his cheeks, and the side of his head was all blood. But the amazing thing was his face. His expression. It was so peaceful, so...released at last. It was then I understood, something I don't think even Tamara understood as much as I did at that moment. All of them are looking for that release, all of them who are dedicating so much energy to hiding what they are, keeping it separate from the vanilla world. I can help. What is a sub but a person who wants to return to the bosom of an All-Powerful Mistress or Master, be watched over and cared for? Sometimes, I wish it was me. I imagine it is me, and I can be like them, at peace. But I'm a Mistress, and it's up to me to take care of a sub, help

them find pleasure through pain, release through death. It follows and fits, don't you see?

"'There is Another who is over us all, over us and over Him.' Just as Bambi said. I am the 'Other' who can make things right for people like my love, my Thomas. We're all afraid to embrace death, even when we know it's the best thing for us. I could have helped him, so he never had to experience that awful moment with his parents. I could have released him and revealed his truth to them, so they would at last know, as he always wanted them to, but not be around to see their rejection or pain from it. He didn't have to suffer, none of you do.

"Struggle all you want, love," she noted the tensing of his muscles. "Those are lag bolts, holding that into an oak floor with solid sub-flooring beneath. Tyler entertains all sorts of guests here, drives them near insane, so he's made it strong. You'd have to be Superman to get that loose."

She rose, went to Jonathan. Mac shouted around the gag, tried in some way to communicate to Powell the fatal mistake he was about to make, fought the chains, the bench, shoving off with his knees, his thigh muscles straining. Powell glanced over at him, then his attention was caught by his Mistress as she fondled him. He had stripped down, so now he was as naked as Mac. Being naked in the same room with Powell was a nauseating experience all by itself, but as Mac strained at his bonds, the lingering after-effects of the drug they had given him only made him dizzier.

Kiera cuffed Jonathan's right hand, locking it to the cross, bent and did the same to his right foot, completing the process of making him helpless.

She came back to Mac, freed his gag with a rough jerk. "You can tell Jonathan what it is you wanted to say, now that I've gotten you all nicely trussed."

"You might as well kill us both and be done with it," Mac spat out blood, regretting that he just missed her boot. "Violet isn't coming."

"Of course she's coming. I expected her here already."

"Violet was involved in a car accident early in the week. She went to visit her mother today."

Kiera stared at him a long moment and Mac pulled his lips back in a feral grin. "Really messes up your plans, doesn't it?"

"You're lying," she said flatly, though there was a seed of doubt in her eyes. "If that was true, you wouldn't have told me, to buy you more time."

"Unless I'm just sick of listening to your babbling rationalizations of why it's okay to murder people in cold blood." Mac weighed his options and made his choice. Kiera wasn't going to believe anything except what would take her by surprise. "Violet is a cop, like me, Kiera. She shot someone in the line of duty this week. You'd have heard about it on the news. Remember, the highway driver killed by a state trooper? That trooper was Violet. She got a flesh wound and she's on desk duty all week. Tyler probably didn't know she wasn't back at work yet."

"Liar!" She seized the cat and Mac ducked his face automatically, protecting himself as she brought it down. It caught his ear, shoulder, the back of his neck, one cheekbone. The smell of his own blood, the burning pain of his back, all of it was adding to the nausea. *If I'm going to die, let's get on with it before I have to throw up on myself.*

"Why won't you understand that I'm trying to help you, release you from your pain? The hiding?"

"Because I accept who I am, Kiera," Mac snapped. "Unlike you and your dead boyfriend, I realized a long time ago that being a sub is just part of who I am. An important part, but not all of it. I enjoy serving a Mistress's pleasure, as much as I enjoy being a cop, or watching a Buccaneers game, or spending a day out in the Gulf on my boat. Being a sub doesn't make me less of a man. And to Violet, it makes me more of one, more of what she wants.

"All you're doing is making excuses. You're killing because you can't stand your own pain. Your sister fucked up your head early and you're acting out. It's not about you playing God, it's about the kill. Just seeing my blood is starting to make you shake. I can see it."

"What the hell is going on?" Jonathan demanded.

"Well, welcome to the party at last," Mac said derisively. "She's going to shoot us both in the head and make it look like Tyler did it. I'm a homicide cop and I've been tracking her. She's killed three other guys this past six weeks the same way. She'll call your parents after she does it, to make sure your nearest and dearest know what you are." He raised a brow, blinked against the blood running down into his eye. "Do you want my mother's phone number? Oh, sorry, that will mess you up further, because my mother died some time ago."

Thank God, because this would kill her.

"Shut up!" Kiera struck out again. This time her aim was wild, hitting him a glancing blow on the shoulder. She dropped it, turned to a cabinet and pulled out her gun, a polished nine millimeter, a Walther P99. A neat little gun to make a neat hole in his head. Mac forced himself to

keep his eyes open as she jammed the barrel against his temple, her trembling finger on the trigger.

"Jesus Christ." Powell yanked against his bonds. "Jesus. I don't want any part of this. Kiera, Mistress…"

"Oh, do shut up." Kiera turned the pistol toward him.

"No," Mac snapped, with enough thunderous force to snatch her attention back to him. "Why kill him first? He's not going to tell anyone about you, a self-centered bastard like him. You want him to suffer, remember? Then he should live."

She hesitated, uncertain, and the gun turned back toward Mac. "I should just kill you," she said slowly. "You're the one who needs release. You're too angry. I can feel how much pain you're in."

Most of it from that damn cat, he thought dryly. "Do it," he urged, his eyes glittering, focused on her, focused on the gun. "Do it and let him go."

"Mackenzie." A voice came down to them from the top of the stairs. "You know better than to give a Mistress orders. I've taught you better than that."

Chapter 21

Son of a bitch, son of a bitch, son of a bitch. Mac would have said it out loud if he thought it would help.

He turned his head over, fighting the sick waves of pain rolling over him. Violet stood at the entrance to the dungeon in street clothes.

"You're not dressed for the occasion," Kiera said, her gaze and the gun swinging toward Violet as his pixie made her way, one casual step at a time, down the stairs.

"I had thought to change upstairs, but I wanted to come down here and see what I was missing. Apparently, quite a lot."

"You stop right at the bottom, and you keep your hands where I can see them. You ruined it, Mac," Kiera said, though she never took her eyes off of Violet. "If you hadn't made me pull the gun, we could have had some fun first.

"I want you to take off your clothes," she told Violet. "Strip down to your underwear, so I can be sure you're not carrying anything, and move slowly. I hate to order a Mistress, but I've got to see this through, you see?"

She backed up as Violet reached the bottom of the stairs, keeping the gun trained on the smaller woman at chest level. That fragile network of curves, flesh and muscle, the vital organs beneath. Panic gripped Mac, caught him up as it hadn't since he was an unarmed rookie in the middle of a domestic fight, a baby in a crib

two feet away while the drunk father waved a loaded .38 at the teenaged mother. He had managed that. He would manage this. He would not let Kiera kill Violet. It wasn't going to happen. He made it so in his mind, made it so in his resolve, let it coat him like armor.

"There are only the dungeons for us, Violet." Kiera's eyes were expressive, appealing. "We're like medieval torturers who can only live with the prisoners, dispensing pain and release, never letting the world above see who we all really are because they can't bear our truth."

"Wrong." Violet took the final step down. "I want Mac. In The Zone, out of The Zone. I want to eat dinner with him, watch him shave in the morning, listen to him yell at the political pundits on TV. I want to nag him to mow the yard, and wake up curled up next to him in the early morning." Her glance went to Mac, lingered on his back, the hot fury of her reaction piercing through him, though she kept her voice admirably even. "I want that as much as I want to have him chained for my pleasure in a bedroom. I want him to be there for me, with me. I want him to take care of me, and I want to take care of him. Don't you want that, Mac?"

He locked gazes with her. "Absolutely, sugar."

For a remarkable second, it was just the two of them in the room, all the danger, blood and restraints gone. Then they came back, as Violet shifted her attention to Kiera. "The dungeon is only one part of it, Kiera, as Mac told you. You had one situation that went bad. You could have found someone else if you hadn't given up."

"He won't accept you that way. He's a cop. He can't take you out into the light of a normal relationship."

"Wrong," Mac said. "I can, and I have."

"Your shirt," Kiera snapped. "Now."

"You don't have to do this," Violet said, slowly toeing off her shoes, pulling her shirt out of the waistband of her jeans. "This can't end well, Kiera. It's gotten out of your control."

"Oh, please," Kiera chuckled. "If there's anyone who understands the presence or absence of control, it's Mistresses like us. I've been neck-deep in the practice of it since I was a teenager. You're a rank amateur."

"A Mistress is born, not made," Violet returned. "You're not a Mistress, Kiera. You never were. You're your sister's sub, which makes me the one in the room with the true control. If you give me the gun, it will be over and there won't be any more hurting."

"This is the last time I'm going to tell you. Take off your shirt," Kiera snapped. "And save your pathetic two-hour class in police psychology."

Her finger had moved off the guard back to the trigger. Mac heaved against the bench, heard wood groan.

Kiera shot him a glance. "Give it up, Mac. This is over. If she hadn't been a cop, if she hadn't known, we could have had so much fun with you gagged. I was going to let her play, let her get you and her off one more time. We might even have let Jonathan do you like I promised. You don't understand. But you will. You'll understand when I shoot. I'll see it in your eyes, and we'll all know I've done the right thing. Now, Violet," she snarled.

"Fine." Violet yanked the shirt over her head, pulled it off her arms and flung it into the air between them, a projectile of cloth aimed for Kiera's face.

Kiera's trigger finger jerked, and the gun went off. Eyes locked on the muzzle, Mac saw the gun kick high.

She was going to miss. Violet rammed into the taller woman, sending them crashing over a heavy wooden chair, taking it with them in a tangle of arms and legs. The bullet hit the wall as the gun spun away out of Kiera's hands.

Violet had police training, but Kiera worked out in a gym regularly and had her in strength and weight. When she rolled to her feet and took a martial arts stance, leaped forward and tackled Violet before she could go for the gun, she demonstrated she'd had contact training as well. The two women made it to their feet. Violet landed a punch, but Kiera knocked her back with a hard kick. Undeterred, his fiery Mistress rolled, rammed forward, slamming them against Jonathan's cross. Powell grabbed a generous handful of Kiera's hair, and she screamed, turning on him as Violet yanked a gun out of an ankle holster.

Kiera shoved her elbow into Powell's stomach, gaining her release, and flung herself on Violet before she could get the gun up. She rolled Violet over with another hard kick to her mid-section, taking her wind and making her drop the gun. Violet spun and grabbed her, and they went over Mac, tumbling to the other side of him. Violet landed on the bottom, her head hitting the wall. Kiera struck her, rolled off and scrambled away.

When they rolled over, the bench groaned, and the significance of that exploded in Mac's mind. As Kiera went for the gun and Violet tried to orient herself, he heaved against the bench. Not up and back this time. Left, then right, left, then right.

The anchoring had been designed for the pull of an aroused sub, resistance anticipated forward and back. He snarled, heaved again, side to side, fast as the pumping of

a piston, every muscle screaming, demanding release, despite the awkward positioning of his legs. The floorboard cracked, twisted.

He roared, using the sound to galvanize him to further action. The floor ripped in response. The right side of the bench came loose abruptly, unbalancing him. Mac rolled with it, using the momentum to tear the bench free and coming to his feet, face to face with Kiera, who had just claimed the gun and leveled it at Violet. The roll put him squarely in the middle of them. He kept going, a forward charge, the bench anchored to his front like a Roman wooden shield.

Violet screamed his name. The gun fired. Kiera shrieked as he took her down under him. One wooden leg drove into her left breast, the other under her right arm. The impact to the breast caused a scream of pain. Still manacled to the bench, he had no mobility in his hands, and she still had the gun, but then Violet was there, stomping on her wrist, knocking it away, while Kiera abandoned all training and went after his face with teeth and nails.

"Roll off," Violet shouted. Mac obeyed slowly, fighting through a haze of pain roaring through his body as if his insides were on fire, but his sense of self-preservation galvanized him to get him away from those wicked nails. Violet swung down with the P99 and clipped Kiera's temple, stunning her, but the woman lunged forward nevertheless.

"Watch your feet," he managed hoarsely, but it was too late.

Kiera caught Violet's ankle, yanked, making her land with a heavy thud on her back. Violet's foot caught her squarely in the mouth, snapping her head back, and then

Mac was back on her, adrenaline filling in as his body weakened. He aimed better this time. When he landed, the four-by-four solid polished leg of the bench went directly into Kiera's face, caving in her skull with a sickening crunch.

There was no finesse to it, nothing but clear, brute strength, messy and final. Kiera's body went slack. Mac closed his eyes as the burning in his back merged with the burning in his gut. God, he was going to throw up after all.

"Let me out of here!" Powell screamed.

"Shut up," Violet snarled, not bothering to look at him while she freed Mac from his restraints and moved him off the mangled bench onto his back. Onto blissfully cool tile that gave him a second's respite from the fire in his gut.

"Mac. Oh, Mac."

Fuck. He hurt. His hands automatically went to his abdomen, where the bullet had punched through the board and into his body.

He heard a heavy thud above them and started up, but she slid her arms around him. "That will be the local police. We're here!" she shouted as the footsteps continued above them.

"Likely... soundproof," he reminded her.

She bounced up, loosed Jonathan with quick jerks, threw a robe at him. He caught it automatically, but before he could bolt, she caught his cock barehanded and twisted hard enough to turn him white, a maneuver Mac remembered had been very effective on him.

"You go up and show them how to get down here. Tell them we have an officer down and we need EMTs. Right now, you're just an idiot on a questionable kidnapping charge. You run, and I'll have you marked on

the attempted murder of two cops, you got me? I'll make sure you get a prison cell with the meanest son of a bitch Master you've ever met in your life, whose idea of a bedtime lullaby each night is making you scream in pain."

Powell bolted for the stairs, but she was already kneeling by Mac again. He was covered in something wet. His own sweat, he realized, though he was trembling uncontrollably. The pain was enormous, sick waves of it.

"Afraid you're not seeing me at my best," he said, through clenched teeth.

Her eyes darkened, "Jesus, Mac, if this isn't your best, I'll be overwhelmed when I finally do see it. You took a bullet for me, you jerk."

"Can't...couldn't...have to protect you. Keep you." Her hands were light, like the touch of angel wings on his flesh. "Sorry I involved you...but you did it."

"We did it, Mac. Mac...Mackenzie," she snapped sharply.

He pulled himself out of the pleasant white haze enveloping him.

"Mackenzie." She was very close to him now, her lips just above his. She had the most beautiful eyes, even when they narrowed as they did now, telling him she meant business, and there'd be hell to pay if she wasn't obeyed. "I absolutely forbid you to die. Do you hear me?"

"Yes...Mistress."

"So all that sappy stuff you agreed to, about wanting to be with me forever, letting me nag you, you just said that to buy us time and save your ass, right?"

He managed a smile. "You bet."

She eased her hand under his shoulder, trying to avoid the torn flesh from the scourging, but Violet could tell all his focus was on the lethal agony in his midsection. He didn't even flinch when her fingernails accidentally caught in a welt, reopened a half-clotted wound on his shoulder.

"Oh, Mac."

"You shouldn't...have come. Could have killed you."

"Don't make me slap you around in your current condition," she said, trying to keep her voice steady, though fury and fear were pumping through her in equal measures. "You'd be dead, she'd be gone and we'd have had to run her down before she got someone else. I was at my mother's late, didn't start here until about 7:30 because I couldn't raise Tyler on the phone."

Had almost not checked her messages, God help her. She kept talking, knowing he wasn't hearing half of it, but hoping he could hold onto her voice like a lifeline. "I knew he had left for his tour, so I figured T&K were in the dungeons with you, waiting on me like he said. Though I couldn't understand for the life of me why you would have agreed to go alone with them without waiting for me, unless..." Her voice caught. "I thought you set it up as some sort of surprise for me. To make me feel better."

"Not brave enough...for that. They...twins...always scared the shit out of me."

She fought tears with the smile. "I was pulling up the driveway at about five after nine when your sergeant called me, said you hadn't reported in. I figured something was up. Mac. Mac!"

"Wh-What?" He blinked his eyes back open, but the pupils were dilated, no focus.

Where the hell were the EMTs? She put her hand over his, over the wound, let him feel her touch over the source of his pain. "Mackenzie, I mean it. You're going to obey me, because you've told me over and over there's nothing you'll refuse me. You understand? I don't care how much you hurt, you will not wimp out on me. You hear me? Mac?" She shouted it, and he jerked.

His silver eyes focused on her for the barest fraction of a moment, enough that she saw he acknowledged her words, lingered on her face in a way that made the tears win, roll down her cheeks. His hand brushed her leg, rested on her thigh. "Yes, Mistress," he repeated. Then he lost consciousness.

* * * * *

They airlifted him to Tampa General. When the copter touched down on the pad, Violet jumped down, a step ahead of the gurney. She stayed out of the way, but refused to be pushed back as the EMTs ran Mac across the ground to the ER doors. Nurses and a doctor burst out, sprinted to meet them, falling in with the rapid procession headed through the double doors to the prep area.

The doctor was young, reminding her this was one of Tampa's teaching hospitals, but she was reassured by his quick fire of orders to place an emergency call for the surgeon on duty. He tapped the bracelet on Mac's wrist. "Get this off of him and get him ready for Dr. Hilaman."

"We'll need to cut it off," the EMT responded. "It's got a key lock."

"No," Violet shouldered forward, yanked the key from the thin silver chain around her neck, snapping it. "I've got it."

They gave her room, and she didn't waste time, lifting his wrist and fitting the key to the discreet locking mechanism. Mac twisted his hand away, bringing up the other hand to fend her off. Even unconscious, he didn't want her to take it.

The emotional reaction overwhelmed her, made her vision gray around the edges, the fear of losing him rushing into that vulnerable opening he'd torn in her heart. But she kept it together, leaned over him, shoving the nurse off her. "I've got it, baby," she whispered. "It's me. Let me take care of it."

She felt the speculative looks of the medical personnel around her, but then Mac's grip slackened and she had the bracelet in her hand.

"You're going to have to stay out here, sugar." The big black nurse was nudging her back with kind but determined intent. "Go give his information to the ER desk. That's how you can help now."

"*Don't* call me that," Violet said, her voice trembling. But the nurse was already gone, behind swinging gray doors that sealed Mac away from her.

* * * * *

"I need to speak to a member of Detective Nighthorse's family."

With his thinning hair and unfashionably plain black frame glasses, Dr. Hilaman looked more like a computer nerd than a surgeon, unless one looked through the lenses of those glasses and saw the hard, direct look to his eyes. They swept the waiting room, took stock of all the police waiting there.

"You're looking at them," Darla said quietly. "Mac doesn't have any living family, doctor. I'm Sergeant Darla Rowe, his boss. I signed the surgical waiver. And this is Violet Siemanski. She's his..." She looked toward Violet, standing next to her.

"I'm his," Violet said simply. "Is he...has he..." She couldn't force herself to finish it, not without a hint of hope visible in Dr. Hilaman's countenance.

It had been eight hours since Mac had disappeared into the surgery. She felt Darla's frozen stillness beside her, of those behind them. His immediate co-workers, Detectives Consuela "Connie" Ramsey and Martin Suarez, and a waiting room full of cops. It seemed like Mac's entire squad had emptied out to share the vigil. As if by being present, they could convince Fate to swing in the fallen man's favor.

"No," Dr. Hilaman said, but there was no easing of his expression, no reassurance of any kind to be found there. He studied them, his gaze shifting between Violet's face and Darla Rowe. "I'll talk to the two of you, then, privately, about his condition. If you'll follow me."

Violet walked at Darla's side, not looking at her, not doing anything but focusing on Dr. Hilaman's back and putting one foot in front of the other. She didn't want to hear his prognosis. She had a sudden, desperate and irrational thought that if she didn't hear it, her will alone could make him survive this night.

Stop it, Violet. He needs you. Don't lose it now.

She remembered the night Mac had held her in the tub, after the shooting. How he had kept the demons from taking her over. Well, she owed him the same. She'd hear Dr. Hilaman describe them, and then figure out how to

put herself between Mac and whatever threatened him, drive them off and keep him with her.

Instead of taking them into one of the small anterooms, Dr. Hilaman took them down a hallway closer to the surgery, into an X-ray room, dim except for the series of films placed up on display on the lighted view screens. Dr. Hilaman stopped on the other side of them, leveled his somber eyes on Sergeant Rowe. "I know I don't have to tell you that Detective Nighthorse is in extremely serious condition."

"Violet is a police officer as well, Doctor. We both understand what kind of injury this is."

He nodded. "All right then." He directed their attention to an overlay chart of the human body, pinned up on the wall next to the X-rays. Violet had a difficult time shifting her gaze away from the stark black and white of those X-rays, the shadows and light of Mac's body, to the garish colors of a cartoon-like depiction.

"This is the entry point, through the small intestine. The bullet came in at an angle, and it did significant trauma to the pancreas. The spleen was completely compromised. We removed it. The pancreas is a difficult area to work on, because of the spongy quality of the organ, but we were able to stitch it back together. See this vein here?" He motioned with his pen. "This is the splenic vein. It's a tributary into which a number of veins flow from the spleen, pancreas and parts of the stomach. It, too, was badly damaged and had to be repaired, as well as a whole series of smaller arteries."

"He's not out of the woods yet." Darla spoke in a wooden voice.

"Not by a long shot." It was clear that Dr. Hilaman had a learned opinion of Mac's chances, and Violet watched, her tension building, as he measured their capacity to hear it.

"You don't think he'll make it," she said. Her voice wasn't her own. It was hollow, as if it echoed out of the aching chambers of her heart.

"He's tough, and in good condition, but the overall health of the body has little to do with the prognosis for this kind of injury. The bullet and the debris that it forced into his body — wood splinters, fiber stuffing — they made a mess of one of the most closely knit areas of the human anatomy. The next several days will be critical. If he comes through them, there will still be a long and difficult recovery period. A dangerous one. With this type of injury, late complications could arise. Complications that could cause a serious setback, even death.

"If he makes it through post-surgery period," Dr. Hilaman said steadily, "he will need home care, a nurse. A long period of recuperation, likely six months or more, time for his body to heal from the trauma."

"He'll have whatever he needs," Violet said. "Can I see him? I want to see him."

Need to see him. Touch him.

The doctor looked toward Violet. She put everything she could into her expression to convince him. To make him understand that Mac needed her near, that the connection between them, her strength, her presence, was vital.

"You may sit with him," he said at last. "And you — " He turned to Sergeant Rowe. "You may look in and satisfy yourself that he's alive and getting the best of care.

Ordinarily I'd allow no visitors, but I suspect you both would be in there the moment I turn my back."

"And we are armed," Rowe pointed out, without a trace of a smile.

"There is that."

* * * * *

Violet sat in the ICU, watching lights blink, listening to machines beep, to soft-soled shoes slap with varying levels of urgency up and down the hall. The stench of antiseptic filled her nostrils. She hated it. Hated the wait.

Her hand stayed on Mac's, her fingers tight on his wrist, so every thready pulse beat was answered by the sure sound of her own. Though she didn't trust the beeps from the machines, she marked every tone of them as well, jumping at the slightest variation.

The nurse came in as she did every half-hour, laid a hand on her shoulder. "I'm going to need you to give me a few minutes with him this time, Officer. We need to take some readings. And you need a few minutes' break. Go get some coffee."

Violet knew by the tone of the nurse's voice she would brook no resistance. Since she was allowed here only as long as the nurses passed on good behavior reports to Dr. Hilaman, she knew she had to obey.

Still, she had to set her jaw and firm her resolve for several moments before she could release his hand. The power and virility was leeched from his skin, making him look like he belonged in a coffin. "I'll be right back," she whispered to him, pressing a quick kiss to his forehead, savoring the taste of his skin, still living.

At the end of the hallway there was a cramped nook with a couple of chairs and a side table with old magazines. Violet assumed it was provided for those, like her, who were temporarily ousted from their loved one's side for tests or procedures. Darla Rowe sat in one of the chairs. Violet didn't want coffee, didn't want to be any farther from Mac than she had to be, so she walked the twenty steps down the tiled hallway and took a seat across from her. "Are they all still here?"

"Some of them had to go back to work, or home to their families, but they're taking shifts in the cafeteria on the third floor. I've been getting the reports when the nurse comes out, taking that down to them. How's he look?"

Violet met her gaze. "He's still here."

Rowe nodded.

The two women said very little, but as the moments passed, Violet felt the other woman's regard become more intent upon her, and the weight of unspoken words building between them. She liked the look of Mac's boss, and under normal circumstances would have gone out of her way to be nice, but she wasn't really feeling nice at the moment. Perhaps it was that hostility emanating off of her adding to the rising tension, as much as something similar coming off of Darla Rowe.

"I've been fortunate," the police sergeant said at last, her voice a quiet murmur. "I haven't had to do this that often. But when I have, I've always wondered how platoon leaders do it in war zones. Watch their men go down, knowing that if they'd done one thing or another, it wouldn't have happened. Even when you send them out in the line of duty, you still did the sending."

Violet lifted her head. The early afternoon light was coming through the window in the nook, throwing Rowe's profile into relief. She was hearing a tone of voice she was sure the woman rarely used, because a sergeant couldn't afford to second guess herself, not with a squad of men and women depending on her confidence. But the quiet of this out-of-the-way part of the ICU against the boiling activity just outside it, the strain of keeping watch here in separate solitude for hour upon hour, left time only for contemplation and bitter hindsight, apparently for both of them. Violet was glad for the distraction, she realized, because her own thoughts were eating her alive.

"There were other ways he could have conducted this case," Darla mused. "He was pushing himself to the forefront from the beginning. He said he wasn't her target victim, but I think he expected to be made by her, so he could *make* himself her target. He didn't seem at all surprised when she left a note on the last body, telling him he was next."

"She…what?"

"The bitch addressed it to him."

"And you didn't pull him off the case, then?"

"No, I didn't." Darla leaned forward in the chair, propping her elbows on her knees, looked steadily at Violet. "I trust my people's judgment, Officer." Violet saw her high regard for Mac in her face, heard the pride. "What I didn't see, however, was that he was pushing too hard, and he was already tired. He was way overdue for vacation time. I trusted his instincts, but in this, you're right, I should have pulled him off the case. He knew what he was doing the whole time, and knew this could happen. It had become too personal."

"Yes, it had," Violet said abruptly. "He was determined not to have another person's trust betrayed, their life taken. And you couldn't have stopped him from trying, exactly because it *was* so personal."

She was furious, knowing Mac had taken the risk, but she understood him enough to know he wouldn't have let it go down any other way. He was that damn stubborn. "Well, I expect he'll get that vacation now." Her voice cracked slightly. She tightened her jaw, looked toward the window.

"Yes, he will." Darla leaned back in her chair, studying Violet in that way that was starting to get on her nerves, so she turned her head, met the sergeant's look head on.

"Is there a problem?"

"My niece has converted to the Wiccan faith."

Violet blinked. "Excuse me?"

Darla shifted, uncrossed her legs, re-crossed them with the right leg on top this time. "I'm fond of her, and so of course I did some reading on it. It's a very alternative type religion, if you're familiar with it at all?"

Violet nodded, drawing her brow together in confusion.

"It attracts some nasty fringe elements, as the road less traveled often will. But at its core, it's a lovely faith, with principles that draw from…" A smile touched her lips that Violet did not understand. "…from natural law. People live in a very unnatural world, Violet. Those who walk outside the lines of that unnatural world, seeking their natural place, the way their instincts call them to be, they often walk a road of high risks for themselves. Doesn't make them wrong, just a bit braver, or perhaps

more foolish, than most of us." She let her gaze travel down the hall, toward the open door to Mac's room. "I don't claim to understand the path that calls to the two of you, but I do know it's a hell of a risky lifestyle for two cops."

"All relationships have risks, Sergeant Rowe," Violet said at last, not sure what the woman was after, but giving her the simplest, most honest answer she had.

"So they do." Darla rose, her expression unreadable. "I'm going to go make my rounds, see who's still around, give them a status. What should I tell them?"

"Tell him he's an oak. And oaks survive what no one else can."

Darla reached out, closed her hand on Violet's. Turning her hand over so their palms met, Violet laced her fingers with the sergeant's, gripped hard. She closed her eyes, unable to bear the emotional connection and eye contact as well. She just squeezed, and Darla squeezed back, a silent communication of what the man twenty feet away meant to both of them.

Then she pulled away. Violet waited until Darla's footsteps retreated to raise her lids, which she suspected gave both of them the necessary time to compose themselves. Her timing was good, for as she opened her eyes, the nurse came out of the room, nodded at her. No change, a good thing at this point.

Violet rose, went back to the room. She paused in the doorway a moment, looking at him there. He was such a big man, his feet all the way at the end of the bed, those long arms lying pale and unmoving on the covers. That beautiful chest, the hair she loved completely shaved from it for surgery. But that didn't matter. Sinking down by his

side, gripping his hand again, she imagined that the strength and love she'd felt in Darla Rowe's touch would soak into him with her own, reinforce the fight going on inside to keep him with them all.

In the raw clarity that the strain of the past hours had brought to her, Violet knew why she'd been so determined to have him the first time she'd seen him, when she'd sensed he was a cop. A part of her had believed it was a sign, that she'd found the fairy tale, someone who would share her life as well as her bed, someone who understood what she was, who she was. All the corners and rooms. Now, denied his strength, she still wanted him with all her heart, wanted him to live, to be with her, to see if they could make a go of it.

The mother who had held her son through the night when he first had to take a life had died several years ago. The brother had been killed in the line of duty a decade past. She knew they were here, sitting in this room, helping Mac find his way back to her. His living family was right here. Her fingers tightened on him.

She was so tired, but she couldn't close her eyes. Each time she did, she saw it in slow motion, Kiera knocking her on her ass, her head hitting the wall. The struggle to stagger to her feet, her head ringing from the impact. The squeezing panic in her chest, knowing she was going to be too late. She'd thought the terrifying roaring had been in her head, but then Mac had ripped the bench loose by throwing his body to the side and rolled, coming to his feet. That gorgeous mangled broad back shielding her as he charged forward. She'd heard the scream tear from her throat, knew it was not going to stop him. The jerk of his body was the only pause he made, and she saw the bullet

punch out of his back, no more than an inch away from his spine, and thud into the wall by her head.

At the time her mind had shut down, refusing to acknowledge it, because she'd needed all her adrenaline to focus on taking down Kiera. But in the helicopter she had seen it replay over and over in her mind, and waves of terror came with every rewind, until she was praying silently over and over for a miracle, praying for the copter to go faster. Praying to go back in time so she could be faster and make it not happen.

There was no worse place to be shot. Dr. Hilaman knew it. Every cop knew it. But she believed in Mac more than in medical science. She believed in his indomitable will, which had resisted her so strongly from the first and yet kept him fused to her, despite his fears of accepting his true nature. Knowing the alternative was unthinkable, she had to believe he would survive.

She knew now that he wanted her as much as she wanted him. At that moment when she had answered Kiera, when her eyes had locked with his, there had been nothing but the truth of their hearts. No time, no shields, nothing but the simple honesty of two lives stripped down to the last breathing moment together.

"Mackenzie." She laid her cheek on his large hand, rubbing against the coarse hair, the rough knuckles. "Wake up. I need you so much."

The tone of the monitor stumbled, made her heart jump three beats. She straightened to glance at the machine. In her peripheral vision, she saw the nurse in her blue scrubs standing in the doorway.

"I think it was just a skip," Violet said. "Damn thing keeps scaring the shit out of me, every time it goes irregular."

"Well, let's see if we can't make it a bit more flatline."

Violet spun.

It was Tamara, not a nurse, standing in the doorway. Kiera's sister, composed as a cold statue, leveled a .38 directly at Mac's chest. Her finger squeezed the trigger.

It was ten feet to the door. There wasn't time for Violet to reach for her ankle piece or do anything but throw her body over Mac's upper torso, curling herself over his chest and head, her own skull an obstacle the bullet would have to shoot through to get to his.

The first bullet ripped through her shirt at the waist, burning her. Violet flinched at the staccato sounds of shots, her heart hammering so loudly against her chest she couldn't tell whether it was her own heart making her jerk, or slugs tearing through her flesh. Mac's hands moved, confused, scrabbling, his subconscious responding to shots the way any conscious cop did, even if he didn't have the physical ability to protect himself. He found her body, gripped, and she held onto him, kept him covered, unable to move even as she heard shouting, running feet, thuds.

"Officer Siemanski! Violet! Violet! Get off him, move off! He's gone flatline."

She heard the horrible whine of the monitor, would have wanted to cease living herself at the sound if her hand hadn't been curled around his throat, feeling his pulse pounding against her fingertips.

"No, the unit's been hit," a nurse called out above the din. "Get a new one in here, stat. Get a cuff on him. Officer, you *have* to move."

A variety of voices, calling at her from different directions, the hands of the nurse, then Suarez and Connie, prying her tight fingers off him.

Pull it together, Siemanski.

Letting go of Mac was the hardest thing she'd ever done in her life, but she managed it, rolled away, let the doctors and nurses swarm over him.

Falling back to the wall, she assessed the scene. Sergeant Rowe was checking her weapon, returning her service pistol to her shoulder holster. She stood just beyond Tamara's body, which was collapsed in the doorway, a macabre sight with nurses and medical personnel stepping hastily back and forth over her while a doctor checked her vitals, confirming that she was dead. Uniforms hovered just behind him, waiting to lift the corpse out of the way. There'd been no time to wound. The sergeant had taken Tamara straight through the chest cavity, twice, and dropped her. Two Styrofoam cups floated in a pool of brown liquid running across the hospital floor, on a direct course to intercept the trail of blood that leaked from Tamara.

Darla's gaze met Violet's. "Thought you could use some coffee," the sergeant said.

Violet nodded, a jerk of her head. The shock and terror were wearing off, leaving anger. Deep, tear-the-ass-off-the-nearest-fool-willing-to-get-close-enough-to-her anger.

"Why wasn't she being watched?"

Consuela Ramsey, standing at Rowe's side, stiffened at the tone. "Early this morning, a uniform informed her that her sister had been killed. She told him that she was

going to their parents' place to break the news. She wasn't a suspect, Officer Siemanski."

"So someone was careless enough to let her know Mac was here? Did they just pull their heads out of their asses yesterday? And how the hell did a woman who was a dead ringer for the woman who put Mac in this bed walk through a hospital of cops without a single fucking one of them noticing?"

"Officer," Rowe said sharply. "They were in—"

"Why didn't anyone recognize that she didn't belong on this floor?" Violet snarled. "What, Charles Manson could throw on blue scrubs and waltz right through the children's ward here?"

She had started low, vicious, her teeth gritting over the words, but when she finished, she was one step below an enraged scream, bringing a momentary stunned silence to the room, the hallway, and likely to everyone on the entire floor. The doctor on call opened his mouth to snap at her, order her to get the hell out, she was sure, but before he could, someone else spoke.

"Singing... Beautiful sound."

She whirled on her heel. Past the arm of the nurse checking his blood pressure, Mac's eyes were half-open, looking at her through a haze of pain and drugs. In them she saw a hint of that frightening distance that people teetering on the edge of life and death had. But they were open.

Violet circled the nurse, barely managing not to knock her out of the way, and put her hand against his face. "Mackenzie, you hear singing?" She groped to change gears, had a terrifying, hysterical thought. "Do you hear angels?" She looked around wildly to see if they had him

hooked up to a new unit yet, so they could be sure that great heart wasn't grinding to a halt.

He made a noise, bringing her attention back to his face. There was something else in his expression, something it took a moment for her to recognize. Amusement. Amusement with her. His voice was a broken rumble.

"Just one, sugar."

She closed her eyes, put her forehead to his, both hands to his face. She felt his arm move weakly to the edge of the bed, brush against her leg.

"What...happened? Shots."

"Don't worry about it." She stroked his cheek, bent close so all he could see was her. She felt the press of the medical personnel against her, wanting to get her out of there. But this was important, as important to his survival as anything they were doing. "You just have to rest, and get better, because there's a lot I want from you, Mackenzie Nighthorse. I'm not going to let you keep your ass in this bed forever."

"You could...come put your ass in it with me."

Violet brushed her lips lightly over his, nearly broke into tears at the slight pressure of response. The nurse's touch on her arm had become an insistent clamp. "Soon, baby. But let them take care of you. I'll be right here."

He nodded, already slipping off again, but his finger caressed her leg once more. A promise that he'd be back. A promise he would keep, or she'd go yank him out of hell itself.

Violet moved back to the door as the new monitoring unit was brought in with several more nurses to get him hooked back up. Tamara's body was being lifted onto a

gurney. A clean-up crew was moving in to handle the rest, the coffee and blood, as other staff members shooed the cops who had responded to the shots back toward the elevators. She thought to look down at herself, and discovered the bullet that had passed so close to her side and through the mattress had only burned the upper layer of skin, nothing serious. Glancing back into the room at the wall, she verified that Tamara had only gotten off two shots. The one that had nearly hit them, and then the one that had gone wild, hitting the unit, when apparently Rowe had put the first shot into her back.

Violet stepped outside of the room, looked down at the bloodstained floor. "I don't know whether to scream at you some more or thank you," she said at last to Mac's boss and Connie, both standing on the other side of the grisly puddle.

Darla put a restraining hand on Consuela's arm when Mac's co-worker curled back her lip to snap. "Easy. We've all had a tough day. Detective Ramsey, please go with the body to the morgue, make sure everything is handled by the book."

Consuela blew out a breath, nodded, giving Violet a curt look that Violet returned with venom. She knew Darla was right. It didn't make her any less pissed.

"I'll put a man on the door," Sergeant Rowe said mildly, though Violet noticed the fingers of her gun hand were quivering slightly, held close to her leg. "I assume Mac's in no further danger, but the hell with it. I don't know about you, but I'd just feel better knowing the protection's there."

Violet looked at that shaking hand, lifted her eyes to Darla's face. "Have you ever—"

"Not in over twenty years on the force. This is my first." Darla gave a shaky laugh. "My nerves are shot to shit. But I'm glad as hell, if I had to finally do it, that it was to protect one of my own. I'm going to go for that coffee and then deal with this mess. Want to come?"

"I'd suggest decaf," Violet said, casting a pointed look at her fingers. "But I'll stick here. Maybe you could bring me back a cup, though. When you're done." She hesitated, brought a couple of dollars out of her back jeans pocket, reached over and put them in Darla's hand, met her gaze. "My treat."

Darla closed her fingers over Violet's, held there a moment. Nodded and turned toward the elevators.

"Oh." She stopped halfway there, turned back. "You know, that was an amazing and selfless thing you did. You better have a good pair of running shoes."

"How's that?"

The sergeant cocked a brow. "Knowing Mac, when he gets out of that bed and finds out what you did to protect him, he's going to chase you down and have your hide."

"He won't have far to go," Violet said, managing a tired smile. "I'll be right here."

Epilogue
Nine months later

Paperwork had kept her late, so the flicker of relaxing candlelight on the back screened porch should have been a welcome sight as Violet took the Stealth over the marsh bridge to their street. Instead, for just a moment, she was torn between wanting to go in and bury herself in his arms, and turning the car around and driving it as fast and far as she could, to outrun the ache that had been growing in her chest ever since he'd returned to active duty a couple weeks ago.

"Damn it, get over it," she snapped.

She pulled up next to his bike and noted that the Aztec lilies she had planted were coming into their second blooming of the summer. Bright, vibrant, passionate red. She had a sudden urge to rip them out of the ground. Instead, she worked her fingertips into the tightness in her temples, staving off the headache, taking a deep breath before she got out of the car.

Once in the house, she tossed her keys on the kitchen table and gave Boscoe his required ear scratching before she blocked out the jumble of emotions, composed herself the same way she did right before she went to work, and headed for the back porch.

Mac rose from his hammock chair, his smile easy but his eyes showing his concern, and she knew she wasn't masking her feelings well enough. He touched her face, curling a loose auburn strand back behind her ear,

brushed his lips across hers. She fought back the urge to devour that firm mouth, to press her nose against him and just inhale all of him into her.

"Good day?" he asked, pulling off his wire-framed reading glasses. A very sexy accessory she hadn't even known he used until she had moved in here six months ago to oversee every halting and occasionally harrowing step of his return to health.

During that period, Violet learned that time could be slowed down and valued, one tick of the minute hand after another. Insurance and the same family trust fund that had paid for her Stealth paid for a home nurse when he was allowed to leave the hospital, but she took over the evening shifts, effectively moving into his home.

Boscoe staked out a spot on the sofa and became Mackenzie's watchdog when she wasn't around. She planted mums by his door in the fall, set a poinsettia on the kitchen table at Christmas and held Mac's head in her lap when he fell asleep on the sofa at nine-thirty on New Year's Eve night.

There were many times that the powerful man she loved had been filled with rage at the weakness that barely got him to the bathroom on his own. When it got to be too much, he took out that anger on her, the nearest target. In return, her fear would goad her to tear his ass apart verbally when he did too much and wore himself out.

But then one day the tide turned, and she saw him start to grow stronger. He began to do desk work for his job, investigative work, and returned to working out with weights to build up a body that had gone lean and gaunt from the months of recovery. She would come home and find him sweating and tired, but with a triumphant gleam in his eyes that told her he was getting better.

They made love several times then, carefully, gently. But she was afraid to do more, demand more. Over the nine months it took him to recuperate, D/s was an area they did not touch. He had reclaimed the bracelet, asked for it the moment they would let him wear jewelry in the hospital again, but she had not moved to reclaim the rights that went with it.

She couldn't initiate it. She didn't know why, because she knew the longing was still there in her, but she had no emotional strength to face what it was that was keeping her from going there with him. When they made love, she sensed a hesitance in him, as if he was waiting for something from her, but she turned away from it, squelched it with the passion of vanilla lovemaking, and stopped the topic from coming up.

"Good enough," she responded, taking a seat across the side table from him, close enough that they could link hands as they always did, establishing a loose connection. He poured her a glass of wine, and then he surprised her by bending over, untying the canvas sneakers she'd changed into before she came home, and taking them off, his hands gently taking her feet up to his lap to massage them.

"Mmmm." She made the casual noise of pleasure, but her gaze was riveted on the way those long-fingered hands moved over her arches, caressed her toes. The way his T-shirt stretched over his shoulders as he bent to remove her shoes. "We stopped a car carrying a kilo of coke this afternoon, but they're trying to get off on a technicality. You heard about that?"

"On the radio." He nodded at the police issue he kept just inside the door of the house. "Caught the tail end of it

when I got home. George was an idiot, searching the car the way he did."

"So do you think we have a chance of making the bust stick?"

As he gave her his opinion, she put her lips to the glass, let her eyes fall shut. That deep, melodic voice, the joy of being able to listen to every syllable, set off an odd trembling deep in her stomach, a need so strong it spread through her limbs.

She didn't know when the words disappeared. His voice just became the music her soul yearned to embrace, to compose the right notes to make their songs come together again, as easily and beautifully as they had before.

His hands touched her face, and her eyes jerked open. She stared at him, leaning over her, and he lifted his hand, showing her the tears from her eyes wetting his fingers. He studied her, and she saw something in his expression, something that made the ache spread.

"I'll go check on—"

"No, you won't. Come here, sugar," he murmured.

Before she could object, he had his arms around her and he pulled her over onto his lap, cradling her. She knew he had built up his strength again, but it was surprising to feel how much, because she hadn't availed herself of it. For so long, she had been focused on the areas of his health that needed bolstering. Her body tightened in need and want in a way she had not permitted it to do for some time.

"Let it go, Violet," he said softly against her hair. "I swear to God, if you don't, I'm going to slap you around."

She shoved against him, trying to get away, and he simply yanked her back. She struck at him and he blocked her, capturing her arms, proving without a doubt he'd regained his physical supremacy over her. She punched and pummeled, shouted at him, and he hung on grimly, until words became curses and curses became tears.

At last, when Mac thought he was going to have to shake it from her, great racking sobs tore out of her chest. She collapsed against him, too exhausted to fight anymore. *Thank God.*

It was the hardest she'd ever cried in her life, Mac was sure. What was more, he knew the cause of every single tear that dampened his shirt front.

For nine months, he had watched her suppress every tear, every complaint, every worry for him behind an inhuman level of energy focused on making him better. Now, at last, she cried for each awful moment since that terrible night in the dungeon. For every time she'd been vicious to him to make him take his medications. Every countless instance she'd bullied, coaxed or teased him into resting so he wouldn't kill himself with the frustration of inactivity. All the times he'd felt her lie awake for hours next to him, barely breathing herself as she'd kept a hand on his chest. Her terror that he would leave her in the night had been a palpable thing. Too weak to hold her or comfort her, at times he'd wished he could die, just so he wouldn't cause her such pain.

But she wouldn't let him, and he learned that a person could love too much. She had shut down her own emotional and physical needs so effectively that she didn't know how to get them started up again. His going back to active duty had been the catalyst for her deteriorating temperament, the reason as obvious to him as it was

incomprehensible to her. Well, he was better now, and he wasn't having any more of this bullshit.

She had soaked his T-shirt. When she ran out, ran down to hiccupping sobs, he removed the garment so her cheek wouldn't be against the wet. He used a dry portion of the cloth to wipe her running nose, dab at her eyes. She watched him as he did it, her beloved face confused and young. Pushing her head back beneath his chin, he coaxed her into nestling her cheek against his bare skin.

They quietly watched the sun go down. He didn't say anything, simply stroked her back, her neck, her hair. Her hand crept over the scar on his belly, her other palm around his back, on the marks of the lash that would always be there.

He lifted his head, brought his hand to her jaw and made her look into his eyes. "It's over, Violet," he said, and his voice was rough. "Don't let it take any part of what we were from us." He caught her hand from his stomach and bit her fingers, not gently. "I'm yours. I never stopped being yours." He kissed her lips, hard, willed her to nip at him as she had done once. When she would have turned her head away, shielding her reaction, he caught her chin in a hard grip, yanked her face back to his. Saw a flash of temper.

"I didn't die, because you ordered me not to. You don't get more 'yours' than that. I wear your collar." He raised his arm, showed the bracelet to her. "Because I want you more than I've ever wanted any fucking thing on earth. So don't deny me any part of yourself, and goddamn it, accept me again. Let me please you, Mistress. Tell me what you want."

Her throat worked, but he didn't see tears. He saw a glimmer of something, something he had hoped to see for nine of the longest months of his life.

"I love you, Mackenzie," she said at last.

"I know that."

She smiled, a tentative gesture, but genuine. "Arrogant jerk."

His hand slid down her shoulder, grazed the side of her breast. During the summer, she always changed out of her uniform before she came home from work, so she wore thin cotton drawstring trousers and a cropped halter top. He placed his palm on the bare expanse of her stomach and moved up, taking up the hem of her loose shirt, sliding it until her left breast was uncovered, displaying the lace of her bra cup. His fingers traced the nipple beneath, and then he pushed the cup down and lowered his head to suckle her. His hand came around to her ribcage, to hold her firmly to his mouth, and she laid her hand on his head, tugging on those curls as his head moved.

"Mackenzie..." she murmured, her thighs loosening, wanting him, aching for what she felt going on beneath her squirming buttocks. She wanted him so much, she was just so afraid...

"Damn it, Violet. I'm yours. I'm *yours*." And in his frustration, he scored her with his teeth, caught the side of her breast, goading her.

Something cracked within her, something that was pain and joy both, a bright, excruciating light, merciless in its heat and power. It felt like a granite wall breaking up inside her body, pummeling the softest, most vulnerable parts of her.

She caught his face, pulled it away from her, met flashing silver with her own determined gaze. "Then fuck me, Mackenzie. Take me. Make me as much yours as you are mine. Leave your mark on me, be as rough as you've wanted to be all these months. Let me feel the animal in you I've always known is in there."

They stared at each other for a long moment. The sun was melting on the horizon, a flood of orange fire that glinted off the light in his eyes and matched what was rolling through her blood, flame hot as the purifying depths of hell.

There was a moment of hesitation, but only a moment. Abruptly he was out of the chair, taking her with him, and he spun her, shoving her down onto her belly on the mosaic table. "Spread open for me then, sugar," he whispered. She gasped as he ripped the seam of her loose pants and the panties beneath in one tear, exposing her to the humid air, relieved only by the lazy turns of the ceiling fan above them. She had a moment to adjust her knees before his foot was against her instep, knocking her feet out wider, a cop move that made her instantly, gloriously wet. His arm snaked around her waist and he yanked her back against him, her hips in the air, her feet leaving the floor, toes not even brushing. She caught hold of the rough grooves in the table surface, the pads of her fingers holding on, looking for an anchor, but there was none but him.

He sheathed himself in her. Hard, brutal, shoving home into her like the slamming of a magazine into the stock of an automatic. She screamed at the combination of pain and pleasure, and knew how much she had missed this, the desperate urgency of a powerful man. Her powerful man. He pulled all the way out, stroking her clit

with his broad head, then slammed into her again, jerking her body forward on the table.

"That's your cock, Mistress," he gasped. "Take every goddamned inch of it and scream for mercy, because I'm not feeling merciful. All I want is to feel that sweet pussy of yours sucking on me until eternity crashes down on us."

It was absolution. Because she felt it from him, all of a sudden she understood it, understood why she hadn't been able to let go, embrace him again as she'd wanted to do. It was so absurdly obvious.

She'd blamed herself. She thought she should have been faster, better. She was supposed to keep him safe. He was giving her the punishment she wanted, stroking away the pain while offering her the gift of himself, a complex give and take she was helpless to explain. With every stroke, she knew he was telling her that, come hell or high water, she was his Mistress.

His hands cupped her breasts, gripped them in his long palms, used that grip to increase the impact of each hard thrust into her, squeezing her nipples between the fingers of both hands.

"You've got a beautiful ass, Mistress," he muttered. He lifted her up higher so it was arched high in the air as his cock continued to pound into her relentlessly, her feet dangling. She was leaving nail marks on the table.

"You'd rather sink those little claws into me, I know." His breath was hot over her ear. "And you will. Again and again, until I carry your scars on my back and I'll be proud as hell of them. But tonight you'll wear my mark."

She sucked in a gasp as his teeth sank into her shoulder, quick, precise, deep, and the pain surged through her blood like a sweet drug. He held on, like a

stallion holding a mare in place with his strength. God, she couldn't believe how much she'd missed his strength, that strength that could mesmerize her, but was also all hers to command.

The climax built higher and hotter than the hottest Florida sun, and she was whimpering with each stroke, unable to get a purchase on the table, not wanting one, but feeling out of control, rushing at breakneck speed to where they were going. All her fear and guilt were being swept away before physical response, and her breath was harsh and loud as the slap of his thighs against the backs of hers. His fingers dipped, caught her clit and began to manipulate it.

"Oh, no..." She went over the crest like a rocket, her hand clinging to his other arm, now anchored firmly just above her breasts. Her body strained forward, unable to do anything but convulse in the throes of the strong climax as he brought her down on him again and again. His thighs quivered, his breath rasped, and she cried out with him again as he shouted out his release. His cock worked inside her like the power of life itself, virile and potent, creating mysteries beyond the desire for knowledge, taking them into the realm of blind faith.

She clung to him, let him make her serve his cock until he chose to slow, until her cries became soft, mewling whimpers. At length, he eased her forward so she was flat on the table, his knuckles rubbing a soft caress between her shoulder blades as her deep pants slowed into soft sobs, quiet hitching breaths.

He leaned down and placed a soft kiss in the center of her back, dwelling there, a tender, rubbing caress.

"My Mistress is generous, and kind," he said softly. "But she's done nothing to deserve a punishment from her slave."

"It's not a rational thing," she whispered. "I just needed to know...I needed to give you that."

"As I said, my Mistress is generous," he responded simply. She was limp in his arms as he turned her, lifted her into a sitting position so they were facing each other. His cock was glistening with her come and his, and the beauty of his slightly damp, living breathing body overwhelmed her. He fastened his jeans and then lifted her in his arms.

"Should you—"

"Ssshh..." He took her inside, to the bathroom, set her down on the lid of the commode. "You worry too much."

"What are you doing?" He took out a bottle of peroxide, several cotton balls.

"I want to make sure I don't cause you any infection."

She turned her glance to the teethmarks. "I wasn't expecting that."

He went to one knee, dabbed the cotton at her shoulder.

"You wanted the animal. You can call him when you want him." Something in his voice turned her to him, made her lift his chin so she could see his face.

Mac closed his hand over hers, held her gaze. "I've seen it enough to know it lives in all of us, and it's not always a bad thing. You bring it out in me, and only you can harness it. Don't stop being my Mistress."

"It's not a choice I have." She smiled. She placed her forehead against his, closed her eyes. "Oh, Mac."

"I know, sugar." His hand cupped the back of her head. "We made it, and you did it. I love you with all I've got. Let me take care of you again, as I've wanted to, for nine fucking months. Don't be afraid."

Everything inside her loosened inside at his low, fervent tone. "I want to spend my life being your Mistress." She raised her head, looked at him kneeling at her feet. "I want to make you beg for my pussy, see your fine ass every day and know it's mine to do with as I wish."

He arched a brow. "Pretty unorthodox marital vows."

"Was I proposing marriage?"

"Sounded a bit like it. Sounded a lot like it."

"Okay, then. Let's say I am." She tried for a teasing note, but her voice shook. "What do *I* get, if you accept?"

He put down the cotton balls, took both her hands in his. "I'll make you feel so loved and desired, sugar, you won't know where one ends and the other begins. What's more, it won't matter. You won't need to separate them."

"Okay," she said, only a little terrified. "So, how will this go, then? You promise to love, cherish and…"

"Obey," he murmured, a whisper from her lips.

The kiss was hungry and powerful, and she gave herself over to it. To have his tongue inside of her mouth, her own curling deliciously into its grasp, feeling his flesh give way under the not-so-gentle bite of her teeth. To be as rough as she wished, to hear him growl against her with need. When she pulled back, she saw he was fully erect again against the crotch of the jeans.

"I think you have a little trouble with that last vow," she gasped. "We'll have to work on it. In fact, I'm thinking

I might need to take you to bed and remind you who your Mistress is. Right now."

Lord, please, now.

"There's no one I'd rather have set me straight. Though I expect it will take a lifetime." He smiled that smile that melted her heart, started to get to his feet.

"We'll see," she sniffed. "I'm giving you sixty or seventy years to shape up, Mackenzie Nighthorse. After that, I'm dumping your ass."

He grinned, caught her lips in a kiss again, swung her up in his arms. "Try it, sugar. Just try it."

About the author:

Joey W. Hill lives on the Carolina coast with her wonderful husband and a houseful of animals. She is published in two genres, contemporary/epic fantasy and women's erotica, and has won awards for both.

Joey welcomes mail from readers. You can write to her c/o Ellora's Cave Publishing at 1337 Commerce Drive, Suite 13, Stow OH 44224.

Why an electronic book?

We live in the Information Age—an exciting time in the history of human civilization in which technology rules supreme and continues to progress in leaps and bounds every minute of every hour of every day. For a multitude of reasons, more and more avid literary fans are opting to purchase e-books instead of paperbacks. The question to those not yet initiated to the world of electronic reading is simply: *why?*

1. *Price.* An electronic title at Ellora's Cave Publishing runs anywhere from 40-75% less than the cover price of the <u>exact same title</u> in paperback format. Why? Cold mathematics. It is less expensive to publish an e-book than it is to publish a paperback, so the savings are passed along to the consumer.

2. *Space.* Running out of room to house your paperback books? That is one worry you will never have with electronic novels. For a low one-time cost, you can purchase a handheld computer designed specifically for e-reading purposes. Many e-readers are larger than the average handheld, giving you plenty of screen room. Better yet, hundreds of titles can be stored within your new library—a single microchip. (Please note that Ellora's Cave does not endorse any specific brands. You can check our website at www.ellorascave.com for customer recommendations we make available to new consumers.)

3. *Mobility.* Because your new library now consists of only a microchip, your entire cache of books can be taken with you wherever you go.

4. *Personal preferences are accounted for.* Are the words you are currently reading too small? Too large? Too…**ANNOYING**? Paperback books cannot be modified according to personal preferences, but e-books can.

5. *Innovation.* The way you read a book is not the only advancement the Information Age has gifted the literary community with. There is also the factor of what you can read. Ellora's Cave Publishing will be introducing a new line of interactive titles that are available in e-book format only.

6. *Instant gratification.* Is it the middle of the night and all the bookstores are closed? Are you tired of waiting days—sometimes weeks—for online and offline bookstores to ship the novels you bought? Ellora's Cave Publishing sells instantaneous downloads 24 hours a day, 7 days a week, 365 days a year. Our e-book delivery system is 100% automated, meaning your order is filled as soon as you pay for it.

Those are a few of the top reasons why electronic novels are displacing paperbacks for many an avid reader. As always, Ellora's Cave Publishing welcomes your questions and comments. We invite you to email us at service@ellorascave.com or write to us directly at: 1337 Commerce Drive, Suite 13, Stow OH 44224.

Discover for yourself why readers can't get enough of the multiple award-winning publisher Ellora's Cave. Whether you prefer e-books or paperbacks, be sure to visit EC on the web at www.ellorascave.com for an erotic reading experience that will leave you breathless.

WWW.ELLORASCAVE.COM